GOOD STORIES REVEAL as much, or more, about a locale as any map or guidebook. Whereabouts Press is dedicated to publishing books that will enlighten a traveler to the soul of a place. By bringing a country's stories to the English-speaking reader, we hope to convey its culture through literature. Books from Whereabouts Press are essential companions for the curious traveler, and for the person who appreciates how fine writing enhances one's experiences in the world.

"Coming newly into Spanish, I lacked two essentials —a childhood in the language, which I could never acquire, and a sense of its literature, which I could."

—Alastair Reid, *Whereabouts: Notes on Being a Foreigner*

OTHER TRAVELER'S LITERARY COMPANIONS

Costa Rica edited by Barbara Ras
with a foreword by Oscar Arias

Prague edited by Paul Wilson

Vietnam edited by John Balaban
and Nguyen Qui Duc

Israel edited by Michael Gluzman and Naomi Seidman
with a foreword by Robert Alter

Greece edited by Artemis Leontis

Australia edited by Robert Ross

FORTHCOMING: *Cuba* edited by Ann Louise Bardach

AMSTERDAM

A TRAVELER'S LITERARY COMPANION

EDITED BY

MANFRED WOLF

WHEREABOUTS PRESS

SAN FRANCISCO

Published in the United States by
Whereabouts Press
San Francisco
www.whereaboutspress.com

Distributed to the trade by
Consortium Book Sales & Distribution

The publisher gratefully acknowledges the support from the
Foundation for the Production and Translation of
Dutch Literature (Amsterdam).

Map of Amsterdam by Bill Nelson

Manufactured in the United States of America

Library of Congress Cataloging-in-Publication Data

Amsterdam : a traveler's literary companion /
edited by Manfred Wolf.
p.   cm.—(Traveler's literary companions)
ISBN 1-883513-09-x (alk. paper)
1. Dutch fiction—20th century—Translations into English.
2. Short stories, Dutch—Translations into English.
3. Amsterdam (Netherlands)—Literary collections.
I. Wolf, Manfred, 1935–
II. Traveler's literary companion.
PT5525.E5 A57   2001
839.3′13608—dc21   2001027540

5 4 3 2 1

Contents

Preface

THE DUTCH OFTEN SAY that Amsterdam is not really the Netherlands, just as Americans have been known to claim that New York isn't really America.

But of course it is. Though both cities are more heterogeneous than their respective countries, they represent their countries and cultures well. And, like New York, Amsterdam is what foreigners often see of the country; certainly many travelers know the Netherlands (or Holland, as it is usually called) only through a visit to Amsterdam.

Visitors to Amsterdam may well know about the Netherlands' unusual drug laws, the city's Venice-of-the-North canals, and its museums full of Rembrandts and Van Goghs. But very few have any knowledge of the Dutch literary and cultural life centered in Amsterdam, with its flourishing, wide-ranging literature and multitude of readers sophisticated in their own and other languages.

Many of Amsterdam's writers live on the same canal-lined streets as their publishers. In the heart of the city, readers may see their favorite writers or follow their quarrels published in the daily newspapers. Those who seek isolation from this intense cultural scene may end up in unlikely parts of the city, as Maarten 't Hart describes in "Living in the Red-Light District." But it's still Amsterdam.

Long before Arthur Frommer called it "Surprising Amsterdam" and helped put it on the tourist map, the city had a reputation among Dutch people for unconventionality. The Hague, nominally the capital, was stiff and formal; Rotterdam was commercial and—especially since its reconstruction after World War II—modern and faceless. Amsterdam was different: quirky, unusual, atmospheric, peopled by individualists.

For one thing, Amsterdam has had extensive experience with what we now call multi-culturalism. Amsterdam's history of tolerance started during the Golden Age of the seventeenth century when immigrants and refugees settled there in great numbers. Catholics and Protestants have long lived side by side. Jews from Germany and Spain settled in Amsterdam as early as the late sixteenth century and remained a major presence until World War II. After the violent persecutions of Protestants in seventeenth-century France, many Huguenots settled in Amsterdam. Nowadays, political asylum seekers from Africa and the Balkans, along with Turkish and Moroccan guest workers and their descendants, and Surinamese from the former South American colony, have further enriched this cultural mix.

Holland's reputation for freedom of expression paralleled that of England but started earlier. The philosopher Spinoza lived and worked in seventeenth-century Amsterdam. Another philosopher, the Frenchman Descartes, came to Amsterdam in 1634 for its freedom and safety. For centuries, writers avoided censorship at home by sending their books to Amsterdam to be printed.

In the late 1940s Amsterdam became the first city in the world to have an active gay movement; one of its leaders, James S Holmes, is co-translator of a story in this volume. Drugs are not exactly legal here, but soft drugs for "personal use" have been tolerated for decades, as the proliferation of "hash-cafés" attest. Prostitution is legal and government controlled, and is most visible in the red-light district near the harbor, where the women sit provocatively in their windows. (When they are with a client, the curtains are discreetly drawn.)

Despite the endless changes Amsterdam has gone through over the years, such as some minority groups dominating certain neighborhoods, there is a distinct and unchanging look and feel to the city. Stylish, unpretentious, compact—its distinctive appearance is one reason for the city's fame and popularity. In his 1998 Booker Prize–winning novel, *Amsterdam,* Ian McEwan puts it this way:

> Clive took the train to Centraal Station and from there set off on foot for his hotel in the soft gray afternoon light. While he was crossing his first bridge, it came back to him what a calm and civilized city Amsterdam was. He took a wide detour westward in order to stroll along Brouwersgracht. His suitcase, after all, was very light. So consoling, to have a body of water down the middle of a street. Such a tolerant, openminded, grown-up sort of place: the beautiful brick and carved timber warehouses converted into tasteful apartments, the modest Van Gogh bridges, the understated street furniture, the intelligent, unstuffy-looking Dutch on

their bikes with their level-headed children sitting behind. Even the shopkeepers looked like professors, the street sweepers like jazz musicians. There was never a city more rationally ordered.

Other European and American novelists have also been kind to Amsterdam's open-mindedness, but Dutch novelists have frequently brooded about its opposite, a strain of intolerance and narrow-mindedness that haunts Dutch life for all its reputation of tolerance and rationality. Essayists have commented on it, columnists have poked fun at it, ordinary citizens have sometimes fled it. A certain pedantic intrusiveness is forever at odds with the anything-goes mentality the city is celebrated for. Readers of this volume may recognize that pettiness in the uncle in Marion Bloem's "A Pounding Heart" or more pervasively in the tone of some of the lesser characters throughout this book. Tourists won't notice it, and foreigners—generally enchanted by the welcoming attitude of the Dutch—may refuse to believe in its existence.

Although small-mindedness sometimes thrives within the city, Amsterdam has often remained the personification of the antidote. Artists flee here from their small towns; gays, like the boy in Gerrit Komrij's "The Light at the End of the Tunnel," come seeking others like themselves; young people find their fortune here—it's the Netherlands' Big Apple. And often what beckons them is the beltway of canals, the "magical semi-circle," as Cees Nooteboom calls it, the city's artistic and commercial heart. This is where the painter in J. Bernlef's "The Three Galleries" yearns to succeed, only to be exploited, while for Remco Campert's poet in "Soft Landings," it is the sad end of his journey. Here live the glitterati as well as the affluent young we see trying to have lunch in Martin Bril's "Café Walem."

These same younger people are now gentrifying neighborhoods like the Jordaan, which for many generations before World War II was a Jewish and working-class district. Other areas, like Amsterdam-South, a stately bourgeois neighborhood, were once Jewish too. In 1940, 100,000 Jews lived in Amsterdam, and whatever resistance occurred to the brutal German occupation of the Netherlands came mainly from Amsterdam. A number of Dutch Jews were hidden in attics and basements, the most famous of them Anne Frank, the world's best-known Amsterdammer. Although most Dutch Jews did not survive the War, a certain Jewish flavor still clings to Amsterdam, as it does more vigorously to New York, and the number of Yiddish words in common parlance is highest here. Sadly, the excerpts about Jewish Amsterdam in this book can give only a sense of what Jewish life was before the War (Lizzy Sara May, "Business"), how the catastrophe came (Gerard Reve, "The Decline and Fall of the Boslowits Family"), and what painful shards remained (Marga Minco, "The Return"). Afterward, non-Jewish victims, like the young protagonist of Harry Mulisch's novel *The Assault*, discovered how permanent their scars were, and how the life that beckoned in Amsterdam-South, away from the wartime disasters of the boy's native Haarlem, was illusory even for the survivors.

Writing about the War is inevitably somber, but so is much Dutch literature, which broods over its material as if still in the grip of Calvinism. Almost as a counterweight, a lighter genre developed in newspapers, mainly in Amsterdam, an amused, easy-going appreciation of quirkiness and good sense and difference. For the longest time, these columns were not considered literature, but toward the end of his career, Simon Carmiggelt, the master of this form, was given his literary due. The column as he practiced it until his death in 1987, the narrative with a point, the essay with a little story, has been continued more recently by Martin Bril and several others.

Many of Amsterdam's present-day inhabitants would not enjoy or even recognize the quaintly Dutch portraits Carmiggelt sketched so deftly in columns like the one reprinted here ("Chickens"). Time has seen to that, as has immigration. Turks, Moroccans, Surinamese, Antilleans, Africans, and Moluccans, who have settled in such neighborhoods as Amsterdam-East, keep largely to themselves; but the younger generation does a certain amount of mingling, as manifest in Hafid Bouazza's "Apolline" and the stories of Hermine Landvreugd, a Surinamese Dutch writer especially popular among the young. It has been argued that the growing conservatism of the last two decades has resulted from the influence of strict Muslim cultures on the majority culture. Perhaps. But surely a meeting of cultures is taking place, however unpredictable their ultimate configuration may be.

True to their experience and history, when faced with conflict, the Dutch will favor the sort of compromise and reasonable discussion that smooths over as many sharp differences as possible. Whether their hatred of fanaticism and their fondness for reasonable compromise—their dislike of what Herman Pleij calls "shrieky idealists"—will blunt the jagged edges of inevitable ethnic antagonisms and identity politics remains to be seen. Certainly if the Netherlands is spared the travails of the new Europe, Amsterdam will have led the way.

~

Because of the specific requirements of this volume, I have had to leave out such giants of Dutch literature as Simon Vestdijk and Willem Frederik Hermans. Equally, I feel pained at not having been able to include such exemplars of humanity at its best as Anne Frank and Etty Hillesum.

In choosing my material, I have been greatly helped by Victor Schiferli of the Netherlands Foundation for the Production and Translation of Dutch Literature. His unfailing helpfulness and good humor have made my work much easier. I am also grateful to the Foundation for its partial subsidy of the translation costs for this volume. And I am thankful for having been able to work with the fine translators represented in this volume.

Finally, I owe much to my friend Virginie Kortekaas, whose sharp eyes and sound judgment have proved immensely valuable in spotting and solving translation problems. I have also received valuable advice from Professors Theo Hermans and Carel ter Haar, and from my friends Jan Pieter Guépin, Mieke Tillema, and Hans Visser.

Manfred Wolf

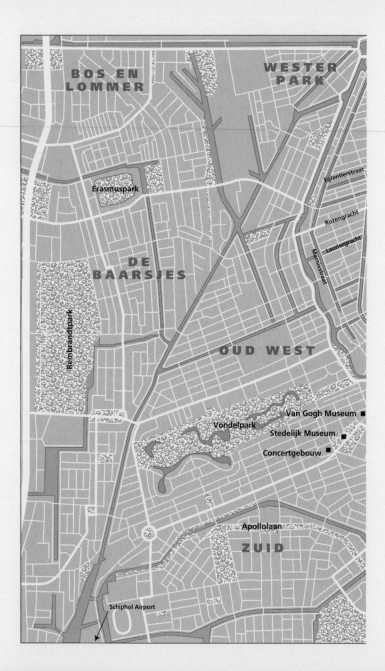

BOS EN LOMMER

WESTER PARK

Eglantierstraat

Rozengracht

Laurergracht

Marnixstraat

Erasmuspark

DE BAARSJES

Rembrandtpark

OUD WEST

Van Gogh Museum ■

Vondelpark

Stedelijk Museum ■

Concertgebouw ■

Apollolaan

ZUID

Schiphol Airport

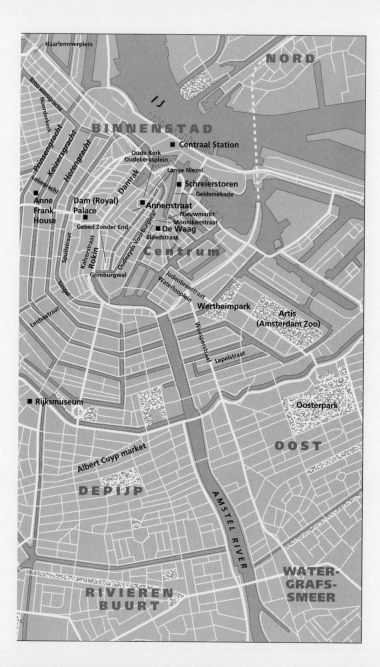

Haarlemmerplein

NORD

Brouwersgracht
Noorderkerk
Prinsengracht
Keizersgracht
Herengracht
Leliegracht

BINNENSTAD

IJ

■ Centraal Station

Oude Kerk
Oudekerksplein

Lange Niezel

Damrak

■ Schreierstoren

Geldersekade

■ Anne
Frank
House

■ Dam (Royal)
Palace

■ Annenstraat

Nieuwmarkt
Monnikenstraat

Spuistraat
Singel

Gebed Zonder End

Oudezijds Voorburgwal

■ De Waag

Bloedstraat

Kalverstraat
Rokin

Grimburgwal

Centrum

Jodenbreestraat

Waterlooplein

Leidsestraat

Wertheimpark

Artis
(Amsterdam Zoo)

Weesperstraat

Lepelstraat

■ Rijksmuseum

Oosterpark

OOST

Albert Cuyp market

DE PIJP

AMSTEL RIVER

WATER-
GRAFS-
SMEER

RIVIEREN
BUURT

Amsterdam

Cees Nooteboom

FIRST OF ALL THE LAND. The North Sea beats against a row of dunes that resists it and rolls, green gray, brown gray, to the place where it finds a passage. From there it whips around the land, between the wall of islands, and becomes the Wadden Sea, then the Zuider Zee. Now it burrows with its mighty arm, the IJ, into the land on the other side. Between sea and sea lies a desert of peninsulas and salt marshes, always subject to the rule of water, protected by pitiful dikes of seaweed, between which the growth of reeds and weeds is burned down so that the land can be cultivated. A region of sparse farmers and fishermen, a population of water people between the streams, the mire, and the flows of water, living on the banks of rivers, on high ground, always threatened by the rising sea, by the settling of the peat, by storms and floods. Thus originates not only land but also a sort of people, a people that neither found its land nor received it, but rather created it. The farmers resist the pumping and pulling of the greedy sea, the everlasting attack, by laying sods of peat crosswise. Everywhere in the low lands the inhabitants lay down dams against the rising water from the east, build houses of loam and reed and wood, and through the first sluices they lead the now powerless water to the sea, which forever seeks to return. If they want to survive they cannot leave anything to chance; they organize themselves in hamlets that defend against the fluid, streaming enemy. The land is marshy and vulnerable under a high, ever-changing sky; the only mountains are the dunes in the west, the Dutch mountains. They have a sea in front of them and a sea behind them: North Sea, Zuider Zee. A river writes its way through the land of Amestelle. The counts of Holland and the bishops of Utrecht quarrel over this wet, uncertain peat bog in a remote corner of the realm of Nether Lorraine. *Stelle:* safe, protected place. *Ame:* water. The land gives its name to the drifting river. The river drifts around the high ground, dances and sways through the land that calls for straight lines; it poses as a slow-moving, baroque festoon. Where it ends in the Zuider Zee, the water is called IJ, and there the river invents a city, a city on the water. Now the game can begin.

The river leaves its sign upon the shore like a seal, writing its form therein like an accomplished calligrapher. Once you have seen it, there is no escaping it: over the centuries, the street map of Amsterdam has become an ever more complicated sign, a Chinese character that has kept spreading but always signifies the same thing. The land is the paper, the water the ink. Like an Oriental master, the river drew the first line, effortlessly, accurately, a sign of utmost simplicity. Now it is up to the people to continue writing. Together they are a calligrapher with a lot of time, all eight hundred years, and the emblem that appears is a neat labyrinth of canals, concentric, crossing each other, a net of waterways and defensive bulwarks, a self-contained cosmos, a magical semi-circle that will leave its mark on the world. The pivot continues to be the river and the water in which it ends, and which connects the city to the world, but in between and along that water the city takes on the shape it has now. Every new line in the drawing is history—economic, political, cadastral. Every movement of the calligrapher's brush is dictated by power relations, wars, economic shifts, discoveries, greed, defense, consolidation. The ring of canals by the sea, forever perpetuating itself, becomes one of Europe's mightiest strongholds; the ships that leave the city and return after many years sail to the end of the known world, bearing the name and repute of the city to the tropics and to the barbaric ice of the northernmost seas and so contribute to the sign that grows.

For what does a city consist of? Everything that has been said there, dreamed, destroyed, undertaken. The erected, the disappeared, the imagined that never came to be. The living and the dead. The wooden houses that were torn down or burned, the palaces that might have existed, the bridge across the IJ, which was drawn but never built, the houses still standing where generations have left their memories. But there is much more than that. A city is all the words that have been uttered there, an unceasing, never-ending muttering, whispering, singing, and shouting that has resounded through the centuries and been blown away again. This cannot have vanished without having belonged to the city. Even that which is never to be retrieved is part of the city because once, in this place, it was called out or uttered on a winter night or a summer morning. The open-field sermon, the verdict of the tribunal, the cry of the flogged, the bidding at an auction, the ordinance, the plac-

ard, the discourse, the pamphlet, the death announcement,
the calling of the hours, the words of nuns, whores, kings,
regents, painters, aldermen, hangmen, shippers, lansque-
nets, lock keepers, and builders, the persistent conversation
along the canals in the living body of the city, which is the
city. Whoever wishes can hear it. It survives in archives,
poems, street names, and proverbs, in the words and tonal-
ities of the language, the way faces in the paintings of Hals
and Rembrandt survive in the faces we see, just as our words
and faces among all those words and faces will disappear,
remembered and not remembered, blown away, forgotten,
yet still present, locked in the word that names the city,
Amsterdam.

A sailor dies of scurvy in Ambon in the seventeenth century and sees once more the city of his birth, now forever
beyond his reach. What he sees at that moment before
death still exists in the way I look at the Schreierstoren, the
Tower of Tears, where the seamen took leave of their wives.
The city is a book to be read; the walker is the reader. He
can start on any page, walking back and forth in time and
space. Yes, the book may have a beginning but by no means
has an end. The words consist of gables, excavations, names,
dates, images. One house is called the Pelican, and would
speak to us of distant voyages. Another is called Spitsber-
gen and commemorates a particular wintering. A street is
called Bokkinghangen, and without smelling anything you
can recognize the odor of smoked fish. A gable shows a
golden portal, but the door underneath is new, so the walker
has to reconstruct in his mind the golden portal that once
stood there. This city is not silent; she hands you the words
—*Melkmeisjesbruggetje, Varkenssluis, Kalverstraat*—and the

walker's imagination sees what history might have told him: that calves were sold in that street; further along, oxen; and in the last part, sheep. A small alley is dubbed Gebed zonder End, Prayer without End, by an Amsterdammer who thought there were too many nunneries in the inner city. Thus the prayer never ended there, and in that street name one still hears the Gregorian chants and the high, thin women's voices. Vijgendam, because the load of figs just rejected by the food testers was used for filling up canals. The walker stops at a building pit and sees how archaeologists strain the dirt, comb it out, dig for the past with gentle fingers in search of signs of ancestors. He is surprised that they lived there, down below. Does the earth keep growing thicker? He wonders whether he could have understood those other, earlier Amsterdammers. Later he sees these finds in a museum. The shoes are recognizable as shoes: he would be able to wear them just as they are. Shoes, bowls, hammers, money.

But the past is not only underneath; it is also above, in the gables with their depictions of whales' teeth, Indians, symbols, commodities, slaves, ships. Everyone, it seems, had something to do with ships in those days; everyone belonged to the water, the same water that still stands dark and mysterious in the canals and that is so much wilder and murkier outside of town, the water of the ocean upon which ships came sailing right to the city's edge, "a forest of a thousand masts." On the old map by Cornelis Antonisz from the year 1544, the walker can see the city with her ships. Very few canals cut through the surface between city walls. The Golden Age has still not arrived, but the IJ is already full of ships. In the place where Centraal Station will one day rise, the smaller ships are able to sail into the city; the larger ones—tens of them—stay on the roadstead. The two large churches stand sheltered between the houses, each at its own side of the water—they are still there. The wide waters of the Damrak came to where the Royal Palace now stands and divided the small city in two: the old side and the new. He recognizes buildings, the layout of streets. The city has saved itself for him; he still walks every day where his house will be built in the seventeenth century and a red mill still stands, the green land encircling the city that keeps jumping over the next canal as it grows larger on every subsequent map. Larger because fame and prosperity rose with the new ships of the Companies. The canal of the *Heeren,* gentlemen, that one first, confirming the might of the merchants, only then the *Keizers,* emperors, then the *Prinsen,* princes. And those other, transverse canals with names of trees and flowers, *Lelie, Egelantier, Roos,* and *Laurier,* in between which, in a district called Jordaan, lived ordinary people: the ship carpenters, the loaders, the sailors, the men with loud voices who brought the air of the great worlds into the narrow streets.

It is gray today, misty. If he closes his eyes, the walker can hear the wind in the riggings of all those ships, caravels, frigates, galleons, brigantines, brigs; he can smell the spices, hear the foreign tongues of the many who have taken refuge in his city: Portuguese and Spanish Jews, Huguenots, Flemish Calvinists, but also loners like Descartes who could meditate so well between the rolling tonnage on the quays; or a visitor like Diderot, who was astonished by "*cette liberté compagne de l'indépendance qui ne s'incline que devant les lois,*" "this freedom accompanied by independence that bows down only to the law." This walk never ends, and the walker reads the images as they present themselves in his mind's eye: the skaters of Avercamp's paintings along the canals, the medieval processions around the Miracle of Amsterdam, the new palaces of the slave traders, those same slave traders chanting their slow psalms in the austere churches, stripped of any decoration by the Iconoclasts, churches we know from the paintings of Saenredam. But also those others, the conventicles of persecuted Catholics hidden away in attics, the hanged girl drawn by Rembrandt, the poet Bredero drowned under the ice, the death of Hendrikje and the auction of Rembrandt antiques, the rebellion of the Anabaptists and their execution, the ostentation and the chilling greed, the weight of wealth, the cheering for one's own and others' kings, the military march of Spanish, French, and German occupiers. And so he lands in his own time: the persecution of the Jews when the city was forever maimed, the places where the heroes of the Resistance were tortured or shot, the entry of the Canadians at the Liberation, an ever-growing history, which this city has inhaled and kept, which survives in monuments and small, almost invisible memorials and in the memory of the living, the words of humiliation and defeat as much as the triumph of old and new victories, a morality, a remembrance.

Evening falls on the city. The lights in the windows of the canal houses make everything look smaller, like a living room. The gentle melancholy of port cities, because the air is always filled with homesickness. The walker I am walks past the Dam Palace that once, when first built, towered over everything. It still stands on more than thirteen thousand poles in the same swampy soil, the soil of Amestelle. Here, in 1948, as a boy, I saw the Old Queen abdicate after reigning for fifty years. Right in the heart of the city, where now lie broad streets and a late tram rides past, once lay the ships. I know where the original Exchange stood, and the later one, and the still later version; where the Waag was, the Public Weigh House, and the Fishmarket, where the condemned were broken on the wheel, and grain was bought and sold. Now I go past the canals where once walked the poets— Hooft, Vondel, Bredero, Hoornik, Slauerhoff—who wrote in my secret language, which no foreigner can read. I walk past the patricians' palaces that have now been turned into office buildings, past the mercantile houses of the lost empire, see somewhere on a gable the splendid sign of the Dutch East Indies Company. Through the dark, low streets of the Jordaan I walk past the houses of the nameless ones of times gone by, without whom that vanished world power could never have existed. Nothing has remained the same; everything is the same. This is my city, a token for the initiated. She will never fully reveal herself to the outsider who does not know her language and her history, because it is precisely language and names that are the keepers of secret moods, secret places, secret memories. Open city, closed city. One city for us, one city for the others. A city on the water, a city of people, devised and written by man and water. A city of all times, and a city in time. A city that exists twice, visible and invisible, of stone and wood and water and glass and also of something that cannot be named in words.

Translated by Manfred Wolf and Virginie M. Kortekaas

Sunday Morning

J. J. Voskuil

IT WAS QUIET BY THE CANAL. A Sunday morning,
early. They walked slowly under the trees in the direction
of Brouwersgracht. The wind rustled for a moment in the
leaves above their heads and then died down again. Their
feet ambled over the cobblestones. Grass was growing here
and there between the stones at the edge of the water.
Where cars had been parked there were dark oily spots. He
looked up at the white cornices gleaming in the sunshine.
A couple of doves were sitting up there on one of the ledges.
They rounded the corner and walked down Brouwersgracht. A man with a little dog was walking toward them.
He waited by a tree while his dog lifted its leg. The dog
kicked up the earth with its hind paws, then, when the man
started walking again, quickly ran after him. On the bridge
over Prinsengracht they lingered for a while, looking at the
houseboats, which were reflected in the placid water, so
motionless that there was almost no difference between the
boat above and the boat below. They descended from the
bridge to Noorderkerk and sat down on one of the benches.
He took the newspaper he'd been carrying and opened it
halfway, gave the supplement to Nicolien, and put his half
of the paper on his lap, though he didn't read it. He stared

drowsily ahead, his eyes half closed against the sunlight. A couple of churchgoers walked past. He followed them with his eyes while they crossed the square and disappeared around the corner. Coming from the other direction was a man with a beard, a child, a dog, and a pregnant wife. They sat down on another bench. The other man got up again, took the child over to the slide, lifted him up, and let him slide down. After repeating this a couple of times, he brought the child back, took a plastic bag, and went over to the sandbox. While he collected all the rubbish from the sandbox, putting it in the plastic bag, his dog jumped in and began digging a hole enthusiastically. The child was put in the hole and the man and woman watched from the bench as he swung a little shovel around. In the church the organ had started to play. The muted sounds filtered through to the square and evaporated in the silence. The congregation started to sing: *Abide with me; fast falls the eventide; The darkness deepens, Lord, with me abide; When other helpers fail, and comforts flee, Help of the helpless, O abide with me.* He listened, moved. When the hymn was over he needed a minute to get his emotions under control.

"Shall we move on then?" he asked, sounding a bit choked up.

Translated by Diane Webb

Chickens
Simon Carmiggelt

THE STORY CROSSED MY MIND again because the passenger who sat across from me on the tram so strongly resembled Mr. Doek. He had been my downstairs neighbor—a civil servant who had something to do with the public gas company, was humble in rank but heavy in stature, and kept only serious thoughts in an unusually high-formed pointed head over which he pulled a black hat like a sheath every time he left his house. Without meaning to, Mr. Doek taught me one of life's little lessons.

He had a small backyard, as barren and dusty as the wolf cage in Artis Zoo. No matter how much he enticed the soil with manure and seeds in his spare time, no friendly piece of vegetation had ever cared to sprout. Even weeds declined. In this little stretch of city sahara was a run he had built himself, where a few dirty chickens, as I could see from our kitchen window, ambled around peevishly all day, their arms behind their backs, throwing out hoarse clucks like nasty old men who occasionally cough up phlegm on the sidewalk.

One day I came in closer contact with these creatures. It so happened that Mr. Doek rang my doorbell to inform me that he was spending his vacation in an undoubtedly despondent village in Friesland, together with his wife, a remarkably fragile little woman who barely came up to his midriff, so that next to him she looked like one of those little fish that follow a shark with inexplicable devotion through the ocean.

"Would you be so kind as to take care of the chickens?" he asked.

I said I would be glad to, and the evening before their departure he brought me the house key and a bag of feed.

"Every day a few handfuls," he said. "This is expensive stuff."

"I'll take care of it," I said. "And have fun on your vacation."

In response, a glum smirk spread over his white face, and he shuffled silently to the door. He did not believe in fun. He thought it was something for small children, like candy canes and puppet shows.

The chickens seemed to have suffered from his depressing influence. The first morning they grouped together like disgruntled sailors bent on mutiny, and when I let the feed rain down in the run, they made me feel I was overplaying my hand. My squatting and crawling around inside the coop to look for eggs in their night ward turned out to be a futile gymnastic exercise, for no matter how much I looked or groped I did not find more than a dirty wad of paper. "Better tomorrow, you hear!" I said. They didn't think it was funny and followed me with suspicious eyes. Not much charm there. But maybe they held a grudge against me.

The entire week the chickens treated me like someone who, under orders from an occupying power, is allowed to live in the best room of the house and, whistling self-consciously, makes his way through the original inhabitants' inscrutable cloud of silence in order to take measurements for the curtains. To torment me, they held back their eggs until they were ready to burst, so that on the last day of my regime the bowl I had put out on the kitchen counter still sat there like an empty gaping mouth.

"By the way, they didn't lay anything while you were gone"—I could hear myself saying to that large, suspicious man from the gas company. He would not believe me and would inspect my chin for any egg yolk still stuck to it. No, the truth was too unbelievable. That's why I went to the grocery store, bought eight eggs, and put them in the bowl. At the worst, he would now think I had eaten a few as a fair recompense for my trouble.

The next day he came to pick up the keys and the bag of feed. He looked just like he had the week before, only he had a Band-Aid on his nose.

"Did you find the eggs?" I asked.

"Yes," he answered. "Eight of them. I was surprised. They haven't laid any for two years now. Too old, you see. I only keep them because my wife likes animals. She doesn't want to eat them, but I do."

He gave me a judgmental look. I just smiled at him.

"Never tell a lie," my mother told me when I was a little boy. At that moment I thought that she was right. But later that passed.

Translated by Virginie M. Kortekaas

The Three Galleries

J. Bernlef

TONY SHORT WAS A CREDIT to his name, standing a good eight inches taller than his fellow students. From that vantage point he observed life at the art school, to which he'd just been admitted, with mounting astonishment.

Before being admitted he had tried to imagine what things would be like at an art school. He would stand and draw and paint from morning till night. Still lifes, Greek statues, live models, maybe even nudes. Anyway, he'd done plenty of those already. Kookie, the girl next door—dumpy, pitch-black hair, cylindrical legs, and a blaring voice—was prepared to pose for him, at least if her parents weren't home. In return she wanted classical music records because her ambition was to become a violinist. When he showed those nude studies and some sketches of ground ivy and acanthus to a lecturer at the entrance examination, the man smiled sarcastically. You can draw, he said in a paternal tone, but here you'll have to tap different sources. Tony had nodded diligently. After all, that's what he was here for. He wanted to learn everything there was to learn in the field of painting and drawing. Etching sounded terrific too. He could sit for hours leafing through a book of Rembrandt's etchings. All those fine lines cocooning the motion of a moment in time; it was beautiful.

He would not easily forget the first day at art school. The school's director addressed the new students. He pointed out that this wasn't an art school in the classical sense, but a "workplace." The students were expected to find their own way around the building and to make use of everything that might contribute to their development as visual artists.

Tony had never thought of himself as a visual artist. Well, secretly on occasion, but it was more something for the future, once he'd mastered the craft.

The man who taught painting was a rough type with a pointed nose and a small silver ring in his left ear. "It's about freeing yourself," he said. "Forget everything you've done up to now and just try to follow the impulse of your hand."

Tony had tried that. His starting point had been a jetty not far from his parents' house. He had intersected the vertical and horizontal lines of the jetty with extended triangles. It made it look as if the sails were freeing themselves from the jetty. Schoors, the teacher, shook his head pityingly. You're still completely hung up on reality, Tony. It's no good at all.

In the weeks that followed, Tony looked in vain for plaster statues, still lifes, or nude models. The other students seemed to be enjoying themselves, when they showed up that is, because when the weather was nice, there were never more than a couple of people present in his class. They faithfully followed the movements of their hands, smashed up tin cans that they then distorted beyond recognition with acetylene torches, or laid patterns of dead branches or broken umbrellas in a corner of the classroom. Tony couldn't compete with this. When Lagerwerf, the drawing teacher, asked him why on earth he was still drawing recognizable things, Tony said: that's how I see it. Lagerwerf shook his head and said, "Perhaps you're someone for Drijver."

Drijver was also a teacher. Tony had never seen him. That was quite possible, said Lagerwerf, because Drijver was based in an annex a few buildings away.

Drijver taught "drawing from observation" in what seemed to have been an old garage. It smelled of gasoline and the walls were covered in black oily smudges. There were some drawing boards here and there. At the front of the garage Drijver had built an improvised podium, where one week there would be a nude model, the next a table with objects, fruit, or flowers on it. Drijver never said much. He seemed to be a gloomy man who talked about the rest of the school as "that place." Because Tony and a thin girl with long red braids were his only pupils, a slight bond of friendship arose between Elena, Tony, and Drijver. Once Drijver even showed a few drawings of his own: carefully drawn bodies trying to fight their way out through the bricks of a wall.

Drijver told them that he had been appointed to teach art history at the school two years earlier but that the subject had been scrapped by the board because of the students' lack of interest. The students had complained to the director that knowledge of the past was getting in the way of their development. But Drijver couldn't stop himself from lecturing. He brought in books for them, they visited exhibitions together or went to the nearby zoo to draw. And in that way Tony felt he was learning something after all. He sometimes dreamed of the etchings of Piranesi, an artist Drijver admired more than anyone in the world.

In order to pass his courses, Tony obediently puttered around with the rest of the group. For instance, he made an African mask with a vacuum cleaner hose coming out of its mouth, a strand of hair in a pool of oil, and a doll with burnt straw stuck on it. In this way he gained his diploma effortlessly after four years. In the last week before leaving the school, they took a few classes with a guest lecturer, Jos Knoop, who gave them some pointers about the presentation of their work and obtaining the necessary subsidies.

In Knoop's view the presentation of your work was of crucial importance. Carelessly framed or dog-eared work had no chance with galleries. And that was the object, to get an exhibition at a gallery as soon as possible because only after three exhibitions did you become eligible for a start-up grant or fellowship.

For two months Tony sat at home looking at his hands. From his room he could hear the screech of the saws in his father's furniture-making workshop behind the house. "What next, my boy?" his father, smelling of resin and sawdust, asked. "I'm an artist," Tony replied. We'll see. Sometimes he thought of Kookie, who had gone to Amsterdam to study violin at the conservatory. Actually Kookie was a plain girl. That's what people in the town thought, but for Tony she was a source of mystery. He dreamed of the fold on the inside of her elbow; how it slipped into the shadows when she moved her bowing arm; how at the ends of her eyebrows a few black hairs tried in vain to rear their

heads; how her lips puckered with effort when she placed
the bow on the bridge of her violin. He started sending letters to Kookie, long, frank letters in which he wrote to her
that ideas were locked up inside him, like flower bulbs
underground. I need a space of my own, he wrote. At home
those screeching saws of my father's and my mother's
clumping footsteps are driving me bananas. And Kookie
wrote back. You must come to Amsterdam. It's all happening here. She'd keep her eye out for a studio, she wrote.
She knew a few painters. She made a joke about his height
and the dimensions of his future studio. Kookie found it
easy to make contact with people. After six weeks she
wrote that she had found a studio for him, thirty feet high.
An old classroom, going cheap. She had also already spoken to a gallery owner, who seemed interested. Perhaps you
can exhibit those nudes. Tony smiled.

The studio was in a school building not far from the Centraal Station. There were artists working on either side of
Tony's studio, but he seldom saw them. He hung some
work from his art school days on the whitewashed walls, set
up his easel, and stretched out a canvas. Somewhere inside
him things were fermenting. It's about the gesture, Schoors
had said, the spontaneity of the first uncontrolled movement. Tony dipped his brush in a jar of ultramarine, looked
for a second through his eyelashes at the pristine canvas,
and set down a sizable right angle. The paint dripped down
the canvas in thin streams. They were like long ultramarine
legs, looking hesitantly for a foothold. He let the paint
finish dripping and put orange shoes on the legs. The right
angle was now walking. He began painting in the back-

ground, a dune landscape with a red and white lighthouse in the distance.

In this way Tony learned to trust his intuition, the rapid, unpredictable smudge that smoothed the path to scenes he did not recognize, but which had nevertheless originated from him. A melting highrise, a hole piled high with milk churns, a naked girl floating into a food automat. He felt as though the bulbs were breaking through the ground, that these paintings were the first flowers of his imagination.

One afternoon he rang the number of the gallery Kookie had given him. The Torch Gallery. Mr. Zwart is not here at the moment. I'll give you his home number, said a girl's voice.

Zwart had a dark lock in his otherwise blond hair. He looked without much interest at the rolled-out canvases, nodded, and took out his appointment book. In four weeks, he said. You're in luck. An artist has just dropped out. A month's exhibiting costs a thousand guilders. There's an extra five hundred for the invitations and the reception. If you sell anything I take forty percent. And oh yes, of course you provide someone to mind the shop during the day, because I'm too busy. I'd like a deposit of three hundred guilders right away, said Zwart, snapping shut his appointment book. Tony wrote him a check. He had no idea how he was going to get the rest of the money. Since he'd arrived in Amsterdam, he'd been living on the dole.

Why don't you ask your father, said Kookie, whose own father was a retired doctor. Tony hesitated. Kookie insisted. She helped him compose the letter. To Tony's amazement, the money was in his post office account ten days later.

Together with Kookie he drew up a list of people who should be invited to the private showing. Besides his family, lots of Kookie's friends who had offered to come and sit in the gallery for the month were on the list. It doesn't matter if I study at home or there, she said.

The private showing was packed. Tony did not know most of the people. An aunt of his bought a painting. Zwart immediately stuck a red dot next to it. Congratulations, he shouted and slapped Tony on the shoulder. But that one painting was as far as it went. Kookie studied études for a month without selling a thing. On the last day of the exhibition he was given two hundred guilders by Zwart for the painting his aunt had bought. He hesitated for a moment, then invited Kookie out to dinner. In the restaurant Kookie laid her delicate fingers on his hand. "That Zwart is a crook," she said. "He originally bought the property so his children could live there while they were at the university. He turned the empty shop below into a gallery. He knows there are lots of people like you walking around dying to exhibit. Well, he'll sell you one. With all the trimmings."

Tony looked at Kookie. "How do you know that?" he asked.

"A painter who's also exhibited there told me one afternoon," said Kookie. "That Zwart has simply found a gap in the market, the guy said. The Ministry of Culture requires three exhibitions before you're eligible for a grant. Right, well that guy got the message. Clever Amsterdammer."

Tony said nothing.

"You must join Arti," she said resolutely when the

tiramisu arrived. Arti? Kookie gave a vivid description of the artists' club on Rokin Way. She wasn't a member herself, but many of her painter friends were. "You'll meet people from the art world there. I'll make sure you get proposed for membership."

A few months later, Tony received word that he had been accepted as a member of Arti. That was another three hundred guilders, which he borrowed from Kookie for the time being.

Arti was an imposing room in which ancient men ate their food messily or tried to improve their billiards' average. The younger people who frequented the place didn't deign to look at him, and Tony was too shy to approach anyone. He often sat at a table from which he had a view of a large canvas of Breitner's.

One afternoon a man with red hair sat down next to him and looked at the painting with him. A stained pocket handkerchief protruded from the breast pocket of his light-gray sports jacket. "Yeah, those were the days," said the man, pointing to the painting. "You should see Lauriergracht now."

Tony took a sip of beer to avoid having to answer immediately. Breitner was a kind of god for him. There you could see it: freedom and composition united. How that man had managed to turn that ponderous oil paint to his own uses. The way he'd painted that horse's bent neck! You could feel the strength of the horse's body.

"Painter too, I expect?"

Tony nodded, without looking at the man. Suddenly there was a visiting card under his nose: L.J. de Goor—Art

Incorporated, it said. 72 Rokin Way. He looked from the card to the smooth-shaven face of the man, who put out his hand.

"Call me Leo," he said.

Tony introduced himself. The man asked about his work, where his studio was.

"Could I come and visit your studio some time? I can't promise anything, but if I see anything in it, your work will soon be hanging across the street." The man pointed outside with an expansive gesture.

Tony had hung on the walls of his studio the paintings he had done in the last few months as well as some old work. It wasn't well hung, but anyone who knew about art would be able to see beyond that.

De Goor was accompanied by a young lady in a semi-transparent peacock-blue dress. Leo introduced her as Marion, his secretary. Tony was going to make some coffee, but de Goor brushed aside that suggestion.

"We'll be having lunch in a bit," he said, lighting up a cigarette and humming in approval as he walked from one painting to the next. "Extraordinary," Tony heard him say to Marion, who took turns looking at her nails and at the paintings. They stopped for a long time in front of a large painting of a cow surrounded by small paintings of meadow landscapes. What was that canvas called, Leo wanted to know.

"The artist is a cow," said Tony. "A free interpretation of Achterberg."

Leo said nothing. Marion whispered something in his ear. "Oh, the *poet* Achterberg," said Leo and stamped out his cigarette butt on the floor. "Very good. Really, very good."

Over lunch at a local Italian restaurant Leo took out an appointment book. Marion fixed Tony with her light-blue eyes. It made his head spin a bit.

"What do you say to mid-August?"

Tony nodded.

"Marion will drop by next week to pick up the paintings."

Tony inquired cautiously about the costs.

"Costs?" That made Marion and the gallery owner laugh heartily. Costs? Now, that was a good one.

"Art Incorporated will take care of everything," said Marion, and she smiled so sweetly that Tony nodded as if it were only natural.

"Fifty percent of whatever we sell will go to us and fifty percent to you," said Marion.

Leo nodded. "It seems like a lot, but bear in mind that we really push your work. We know exactly where the potential buyers are. Bankers, attorneys, dentists, those kinds of people."

"We've got a huge database," said Marion. Now she also took an appointment book out of her bag.

"Does my work have to be sent off right now?" said Tony. "It's only the beginning of July."

"Surely you don't think we're going to wait for the opening to start selling? If a few things have already been sold by the time we open, it attracts new buyers. People are always afraid of missing the boat."

Marion nodded.

Amsterdam in July was a completely different city from
when Tony had moved there in January. The Amsterdammers had left and tourists had taken their place. Tony
was constantly being stopped by people who wanted to
know the way to the Anne Frank House or the "Van-Go"
Museum. The weather was hot and oppressive. In the
evenings there were occasional thunderstorms. Tony spent
most of the time in his now empty studio. His colleagues
in the adjoining rooms had also left.

He looked at the empty walls but simply couldn't get
down to work. Kookie had gone to the Pyrenees with a girlfriend. Now and then he phoned Art Incorporated, but no
one answered or he got an answering machine on which
Marion announced that there was no one there to take the
call at the moment. He never left a message. He didn't
really have anything to say.

Occasionally he leafed through the few art books he
possessed. He admired the cheerfulness of Matisse, the
gossamer-light interiors of Bonnard, the ethereal jars and
vases of Morandi that seemed to dissolve into the light as
you looked at them. Painting is in the service of light. He
had read that somewhere. What matters is to paint an inner
image. That's what the American painter Edward Hopper
had said.

But the light in the studio struck Tony as heavy and sati-
ated, and however much he looked inside himself, there was
no inner image to be seen.

One morning, after he had accidentally put salt instead of
sugar in his coffee, he covered a canvas in dollops of paint.
With a plastering trowel he drew wide lines across the canvas. From the table in a corner of the studio, he looked at the

result. Was this the ultimate gesture, complete spontaneity, not hampered by any intention? He shook his head, got up, and cut the canvas to pieces. Abstract art was capitulation to chance, anonymous and interchangeable. No, the point was to use chance to further your own ends, as Francis Bacon once said in an interview. Sometimes he thought back nostalgically to his art school days when no one had made demands on him and every piffling idea was acclaimed by teachers who themselves could not draw or paint.

Tony cut up a map of Amsterdam, stuck the pieces onto a canvas and painted a naked female figure over the top. It may not have been an inner image, but it was how he felt.

When Kookie rang to say she was back and asked if he had worked well, he looked at the white walls for a moment and said, "I'm frozen." She didn't understand what he meant. When she came to his studio the next day and saw the empty walls, she stroked his skinny arm with her brown hand for a moment.

"Every artist feels like that sometimes," she said. "You'll see, after the exhibition." In twelve days' time. Had the invitations arrived yet? He shook his head. Art Incorporated was never in. But those invitations must be sent off today, said Kookie. Come on, we're going there. Now!

The building on Rokin Way was a stately office block from the period of the Amsterdam school of architecture. Art Incorporated had its offices on the fourth floor. They took the elevator and a moment later they were standing in front of a frosted glass door. Kookie knocked. When no one opened, Kookie pushed the door handle downward with determination. They entered a large light room with a number of empty tables and desks. At a desk by the window, Marion was sitting at a computer screen. She turned around and smiled when she saw Tony looming up behind Kookie. "I didn't hear you two," she said. "Sorry."

Kookie came straight to the point. That's just the way she was. Beautiful Marion didn't like it, you could tell. "Who are you exactly?" she asked. "I'm Kookie," said Kookie, louder than necessary. "I represent the artist. Well, have the invitations gone off or not?"

Marion said nothing and brushed a lock of her blond hair from her forehead. "The exhibition has been postponed. I thought Tony would be on vacation, that's why."

"Where are my paintings?" asked Tony.

"They're out on show," said Marion and pressed some keys. "Here, come and have a look. All the paintings are on view with our clients."

Yes, there they were on the screen, the titles that he had given his canvases one afternoon with a bottle of wine in him.

A liter is a liter. It's not much. After despair the Dairy Collective man. Drop me a line. The artist is a cow. Off work (Holiday).

"At the end of the month we'll contact our clients again. I estimate we'll have sold about five or six pieces. The rest we'll hang here in the gallery in September."

Tony looked around him. A chic office. You had to admit it. A Corneille and an Appel on the wall. Expensive filing cabinets. A bouquet of wildflowers on one of the tables and in a wall cabinet, a collection of expensive bottles of alcohol. Perhaps Marion was right and he must be more patient. Kookie seemed to be hesitating too. "We'll stay in touch," she said.

Looking back at it, Tony didn't understand where he got

the nerve to suddenly ask Marion for an advance of five hundred guilders. Even Kookie looked surprised. The only person who seemed to find it quite normal was Marion. She disappeared into a small office behind the room and came back a moment later with five one hundred guilder notes. Brand new. He paid Kookie back what he had borrowed as soon as they got into the elevator.

August ended, September came. Not a word from Art Incorporated. They didn't answer the telephone and when Tony dropped by the office it was closed. He didn't meet Leo de Goor in Arti either. The barman shook his head. No, he hadn't seen Mr. de Goor for months.

Tony realized that he had given away twenty paintings without knowing where they were going. Who were those clients of Art Incorporated actually?

In the lobby of the office building on Rokin Way, Art Incorporated's nameplate had been removed. Again Kookie took the initiative. She went to a lawyer, a friend of her father's. After two weeks she received a lengthy letter from the lawyer. Art Incorporated did not exist at the address given. Nor was the gallery registered with the Chamber of Commerce. Leo de Goor and Marion seemed to have disappeared off the face of the earth. "I'm afraid there's not much I can do for your client," said the lawyer in the conclusion of his letter, "since your client was unable to submit any proof of the transfer of his paintings." Oh yes, he was sorry.

Tony seemed inconsolable. Kookie felt really sorry for him. First she considered going to bed with him but then had a better idea.

"I'm going to pose for you again," she said, and was as good as her word.

Tony sat at the table in his studio and looked at the squat figure with the pitch-black armpits and pubic hair. He got up.

"Sit over there, on that box. Your hands around your knees."

He began sketching her body in charcoal. Then he asked her to sit on the chair with her legs wide apart. He looked at her open pink labia. Gravel, he thought, there's got to be gravel coming out. Her skin full of pebbles, dust. They must become dangerous nudes.

In a few days he sketched out ten canvases in which Kookie was depicted in increasingly aggressive poses. He would fill in the rest later, he said. Kookie looked tired and drained.

After a week he said she no longer needed to come, to pose, that is.

"I know what I want now," he said.

"Is the bulb finally out of the ground?" she asked.

He nodded.

The next day he took the train to Zandvoort and collected two large plastic bags of shell dust, sand, and pebbles. He sketched Kookie's body in earth tones. He covered thighs, elbows, pudenda, and feet with epoxy and then scattered shell dust and sand over it.

The bodies now looked as if they had just been excavated. They were ugly, repulsive paintings. The uglier and more repulsive they got, the more pleasure Tony seemed to take in his work. While he filled up the dark shapes of her body—which seemed to be abandoning itself to attacks of colic and spasms—with dust and gravel, he played Mozart's Requiem and Mahler's Ninth, which Kookie had given him as a present, at full volume.

The next day someone knocked at the door. He opened it and looked down at an Italian-looking guy in a T-shirt and jeans. It was the artist who lived next door. He was called Mouse. Adolf Mouse, or actually Mues. He was Swiss and spoke Dutch with a heavy accent. Mouse asked if the music could be turned down a bit, as he was working too, and then, without asking permission, walked past him into the studio. The bog-brown nudes were hanging on the walls.

"Christ," muttered Mouse, putting his hands in his pockets. "That's very sexy, Tony, very sexy."

Tony stood there without saying anything. He had no idea what exactly he had painted. While he was painting he hadn't thought for a moment about spontaneity, the first gesture, or an inner image; he had simply created them in a state of rage and excitement. The sand crunched under Mouse's woven leather shoes.

"Have you got a gallery yet?" asked Mouse after he had poured himself a glass of wine. Tony began laughing sarcastically, but decided to keep the story about Art Incorporated to himself. He shook his head.

"I'm sure that my gallery would be very interested. Do you know the Jak Gallery?"

Tony nodded. He had come across the name occasionally in the paper. "Aren't they in Spuistraat?"

Mouse offered to introduce him to Nico Schaap, the owner. Nico had once been a press photographer, so he had a keen eye for what was topical, said Mouse. He would be completely bowled over by this.

Two days later Nico Schaap, with Mouse in tow, paid a visit. Mouse had not exaggerated. Within a quarter of an hour, Nico was in complete raptures, encouraged by Mouse, who did his utmost to convince the gallery owner of the innovative quality of Tony's work. "More important than Beuys," Tony heard him say to Schaap. "With the intimacy of Kitaj's later nudes. So is it a deal?"

"Of course," said Nico and handed Mouse his wallet.

"I'll pop out and get some whiskey," called the little Swiss and rapidly left the studio with the wallet.

Nico Schaap sat down at the table opposite Tony. He asked whether Tony had ever exhibited before. "Not really," said Tony. "I paid for my first exhibition myself and the second didn't come off."

"Then this'll be your breakthrough, boy," said Nico, with a touch of emotion in his voice. "October 15. I'll have to move back a couple of other exhibitions for it, but this work is so sensational, it takes precedence."

Schaap seemed really impressed.

"You can really draw well," he said. "You don't see that very often nowadays."

"I was taught by Drijver," said Tony. "He didn't want to hear about that modern stuff, but he could certainly draw."

Tony immediately rang up Kookie to tell her the good news. She sounded at once happy and reserved. "They're not very good likenesses, I hope?" she asked with concern.

CANALS   31

"Of course not," said Tony. "They're really inner images, not pictures of your body."

A few days later Nico came to photograph the paintings for the catalogue. He brought a contract with him: Tony had to describe all the paintings and give them titles. Titles? He'd never thought about that.

"Do I have to?" said Tony. He would prefer to call the paintings simply "Painting." Or if necessary "Composition." Language does not belong with a painting. Or at most, language in its most direct, descriptive form so that the description and the painting directly referred to each other. Man in Stable. Woman in Bath. Some such thing. But Nico didn't agree.

"Titles sell," he said in the tone of a connoisseur. "What would you say to 'Gravel Nude,' 'Sand Nude,' 'Bog Nude,' 'Sandpaper Nude'?"

Tony said it was okay by him and meanwhile looked at his paintings. Yes, they were ugly. There was no doubt about it. But they had the attractive intractability of something that refused to admit defeat. In some way there was a visually unconquerable residual value in the canvases, which made women's bodies inaccessible, proud. They might not be beautiful, but they were his, by Tony Short, or T. S. as he had signed each canvas at bottom right.

Not until the opening did Tony see that his canvases were intended to fetch fifteen thousand guilders each. Wasn't that a bit steep? Nico shook his head, put his finger to his lips, and pointed to the men and women who had assembled in the gallery for the opening, glasses of white wine or mineral water in their hands. They wore expensive, sporty clothes. Fox furs dangled nonchalantly over the arms of several women.

Nico introduced him to a number of his "clients," as he called them. The women looked at him uncertainly from behind their makeup masks. The men pumped his hand, as if after they had seen these paintings the best thing they could do would be to tear it right off.

Tony looked around rather unhappily. He didn't know anyone. And where was Kookie? Was she perhaps afraid that people would recognize her, hanging there on the wall, muddy and full of sand and in strange poses? Tony thought he might as well have another glass of the sour white wine.

And by the way, where was the catalogue?

Good question. What a shame, what a shame. The printer had promised expressly. But one of his machines had broken down. It would be here next week for sure. Nico promised he would make sure to send copies to his best clients.

At the back of the gallery there was a grand piano painted in an extremely personal way by Corneille himself. Corneille had a fixed contract with the Jak Gallery, Nico had told him earlier, not without pride. At every opening someone would come up to him wanting to buy the grand piano, but Nico didn't sell it. It belonged with the gallery, a kind of trademark, he said.

An elderly woman with bow legs and a knitted bag entered the premises.

"Ah, there's Marie," said Nico and went up to the bespectacled lady. "Lovely to see you."

She gave a short nod and made immediately for the grand piano. She took off her dark blue raincoat and draped it over the instrument. From her bag she produced a thick music album. Mozart sonatas. Tony watched as Nico took him by the hand and introduced him to her.

"This is the artist, Marie," said the gallery owner.

Marie nodded and put the music album on the stand. "I've put on matching stockings," she said to Nico.

Tony saw it too. The woman was wearing Corneille stockings around her spindly legs. She kicked the floor firmly a few times before launching into a Mozart sonata several tempi too slow. Corneille's garish birds and tropical vegetation brushed up and down Marie's wrinkly thighs.

Many people cast only a fleeting glance at the paintings, after which they left the gallery with a limp wave in Nico's direction. Tony looked at his watch. Three-thirty. Did he really have to stay here till six? And where was Kookie? Nico beckoned to him.

"Come with me to the office for a minute," he said.

Had something been sold already perhaps?

Nico cautiously closed the door of the little office next to the gallery space. "Listen, Tony," he said. "I think what you do is fantastic. But it's not catching on. Nothing's been sold."

"But the exhibition's only been open for an hour and a half," said Tony.

"If I don't sell anything in the first hour, the writing's on the wall," said the gallery owner, lighting up a cigarette. "Take it from me. I know my customers. I'll give you a week."

Tony didn't understand him.

"Then I'll hang lithos by Corneille," said Nico. "They always sell."

"Perhaps you should knock something off the price," said Tony cautiously. "I think they're quite expensive myself."

"You must be out of your mind," said Nico. "They're priced exactly right."

As Tony came out of the office he saw Mouse standing there, in animated conversation with a woman with bleached-blond hair pinned up. She was just putting her arm round Mouse's shoulder in a familiar gesture. That wouldn't work with me, thought Tony and raised his hand in greeting.

"Nicely hung," said Mouse and introduced him to the lady.

"I'm Mieke Straat," said the woman, "married to Jippe Straat, the lawyer. Unfortunately my husband couldn't make it. Nico always has such interesting painters. The other day too. Also such a young fellow. Come, what was his name again."

Because Tony wasn't listening to her, she took hold of his hand.

"I think your paintings are very impressive," she said, "but our house is full of paintings. Nico has seen to that. Believe me, he can sell." She laughed shrilly.

Only now did Tony realize that the woman was a little drunk. Behind him Marie was mistreating Mozart. "Isn't there any beer?" a sonorous voice suddenly rang out. "Hey, Buizerd," he heard Nico shout. Tony turned around. A bearded man with tufts of hair that grew out of his ears like moss raised his rough hands above his head and shook his oblong skull. "And you must be Tony Short," he cried in a stentorian voice.

"Yes, Mr. Buizerd," said Tony.

Buizerd pulled him into a corner of the gallery, which was now emptying fast.

"Marie, softer," cried Buizerd imperiously, who was obviously a regular guest. Then he turned to Tony. "Boy," he said, "as an old hand in the business, let me say a few things to you. It's all very nice, but people aren't interested in a cunt full of sand. They've already got one of their own." Buizerd gave a whinnying laugh and meanwhile took a beer from Nico Schaap, who behind Buizerd's back was gesticulating to indicate that Tony shouldn't take the pronouncements of the old painter too seriously.

"The people who buy here," Buizerd continued his argument, "have just caught up with the Cobra movement. Some nice wild animals to hang over the sofa. Take it from me, next time take a slightly more decorative approach. Then Jak will be able to do a lot for you."

By now there were almost no visitors left in the gallery. Kookie hung there forlorn and naked on the white walls. Tony almost felt sorry for his own paintings. Instead of a month they would hang here for only a week.

"I'll be off to the pub on the corner," he said to Nico, who was just stuffing twenty-five guilders into Marie's hand.

"I'll be right along," said Nico.

Tony hesitated for a minute. Then he said. "Shame about the catalogue."

Nico shrugged his shoulders. "We've got a whole week yet," he said, "who knows what may happen."

Tony went to the Flashing Light pub and watched a basketball game at the bar with a few scattered customers. All the players were his height. Full of admiration he watched the ease with which they deposited the ball in the net.

When he looked at his watch it was seven o'clock. Nico had not shown up. He rang Kookie from the pub.

He told her about the opening. Her reaction was less indignant than he had hoped. No indeed, she hadn't dared to come. Not out of fear of being recognized, but because she thought they were creepy paintings. "To think you see me like that," she said.

"But it's not you at all," Tony had replied. "I just wanted to make bodies that had weight, substance. But obviously no one sees that. Nico doesn't; nor do his customers."

The following week he dropped in again at the Jak gallery. Meanwhile, the catalogue had arrived. It looked beautiful, although the reproductions stripped the paintings of their mysterious protective layer. They had become slightly obscene. Next to one painting in the gallery was a red dot.

"Sold?" asked Tony.

"Well, sold," said Nico. "That painting is for the printer of the catalogue. After all, you don't get something for nothing. But you'll get a nice catalogue out of it. That'll be very important for your portfolio in a little while."

Tony nodded. Yes, they'd talked about that at art school too. The importance of your portfolio.

He had now had three exhibitions in the space of a year. Now he could apply for a grant. That same day he called the Arts Foundation and asked if they would give him a grant.

"It's not as easy as that," said a lady at the other end of the line in a piqued tone. "I'll send you a form."

Tony filled out the form. Have exhibited in three galleries: The Torch, Art Incorporated, and Jak. Live and work in Amsterdam, he wrote, signed the paper, and stuffed it into an envelope with a catalogue. He should receive a reply from a committee within a month.

On the last day of the exhibition he hired a van to collect the paintings and boxes of catalogues from the Jak Gallery. Nico had put all his paintings in the office and was busy hanging Corneille's lithos. Still, he'd find time for a quick one in the Flashing Light, he said amiably.

The bar was deserted apart from a small man with wildly sprouting hair, who was sitting with his back to them and indicating to the barkeeper with silent fingers the tempo at which he wanted his gin poured.

"Better luck next time," said Nico, raising his glass.

Tony nodded and thought of his empty studio, which would soon be full of his unsold paintings and boxes full of catalogues.

After Nico left—"you understand, I'll have to work my butt off to be ready in time for tomorrow"—the little guy at the bar turned around.

"So," he said with satisfaction and a lopsided grin. "Another victim of Nico Schaap." He raised his glass of gin and toasted Tony.

"Do you know Mr. Schaap?" asked Tony.

The man came over and sat next to him. "I'm Pieter Reinaert," he said with a lisp. "Also a bit of an artist, although these days I prefer to drink, I must say." This was an invitation to Tony to provide him with a new gin. A "straight" gin, as Reinaert called it.

"Well," he said, "so you let yourself get screwed too."

Tony didn't understand the drinking artist.

Reinaert made a conspiratorial gesture, as if there were people in the pub who might eavesdrop on them, but besides the barkeeper reading the daily paper and the voice of Vera Lynn and her soldiers' chorus, no one was there.

"Ever heard of the 'interest scheme' of the Ministry of Culture?" whispered Reinaert.

No, Tony didn't have a clue.

"It enables customers of a gallery to buy art on the instalment plan. The ministry pays the interest. A precondition for a gallery to be eligible for that scheme is its policy. Nico Schaap's policy, that is." Reinaert grinned. Nothing had been done to his teeth since time immemorial. "Do you get the idea?"

Tony shook his head and looked rather impatient. What was he supposed to do with this drunken artist?

"The committee that determines eligibility monitors the gallery to see whether its policy is adventurous enough. High risk, they call it, I think. Well, artists like you and me are used for that purpose. The point is not for them to sell you or me. We just have to have hung there. You even pay for the catalogue yourself. Or isn't that so?"

Tony couldn't deny it.

"So that's how it works," said Pieter Reinaert and laboriously hoisted himself up with both hands on the edge of the table.

"The artist is a cow," said Tony.

"Do you hear that, Frans?" said Reinaert to the barkeeper. "The gentleman is fouling his own nest."

The man nodded without looking up from his paper.

Five weeks after he had collected his paintings from Nico Schaap, he received word from the Arts Foundation. The committee, the letter said, felt that "your work makes no contribution to the development of the Dutch plastic arts."

Tony looked at the nudes on the wall. Kookie. Not

important for the development of Dutch art. He felt as if he himself were filling up with sand. That afternoon he dropped in to see Mouse, who was busy filling an empty ketchup bottle with doll's eyes. He asked him if he would look after his things until he got back.

"Here's the key," he said. "I'm going home for a bit."

His parents didn't seem surprised that he had come back. His room hadn't been touched.

"You can move right back in."

They were people of few words. During the day Tony could often be found in the furniture-making workshop. One day he decided to join in. Varnishing. He liked it more and more: applying a shiny coat of varnish to a dull sanded chest of drawers.

One evening his mother said, "Do you know Kookie's back?"

Yes, Kookie had chucked it all too.

"I wasn't good enough," she said. "I could have gone on but then I would have spent the rest of my life in an orchestra. All those bows going up and down in unison."

They walked hand in hand through the Vossenbos woods, just outside the town. They stopped under a beech tree. Now he's going to kiss me, thought Kookie. At last it's going to happen. But Tony just took hold of Kookie's arm, gently turned it outward and then back a little way.

"Look," he said, "that fold, those creases. That's what really started it all."

Translated by Paul Vincent

Café Walem

Martin Bril

A YOUNG COUPLE sat stiffly across from one another at a tiny table in Grand Café Walem on Keizersgracht. The sun was shining in the garden. He wore glasses and a blazer; there was a blush on her cheeks.

"What are you having?" asked the man after a while.

"How would I know?" snapped the woman. "You have the menu."

True. He had been staring at it the whole time. Evidently he still had not grasped what it said. He passed the menu to his wife.

"Actually, I'm not very hungry," she said.

The man took the menu back, scanned the offerings, and beckoned a waitress. Anger and disappointment battled on his face. His wife looked at her nails. She took a deep breath.

"Bert . . ." she started.

"Come on, Carla. I'm starved." He looked with annoyance at his watch. "We have plenty of time."

A waitress arrived. She was wearing tight black pants that fit low on her hips. She wore a black top that was too short. A considerable amount of flesh lay bare at eye level.

"Two coffees with cream," said Carla, in that tone women reserve for other women.

The waitress scratched something on a pad and turned dramatically around.

"Carla, please. We were going to have a pleasant lunch."

Carla sighed.

Bert took her hand.

Then in his inside pocket the phone rang. Immediately the mood changed. The couple now entered a state of high excitement. Bert pulled violently at his jacket to take hold of the cell phone (the antenna got stuck in the lining), while Carla careened so intensely forward that her head bounced against Bert's nose, making it look for a moment as if he would have to choose between the bleeping phone and his glasses, which were sliding down his nose. Fortunately he extricated the apparatus, but he still had to do something about his glasses lest he press the wrong button.

"Hello. This is Bert."

Carla snatched the phone from his hands.

"This is Carla," she called.

She listened for a moment.

"Oh, I hear her, I hear her," she exclaimed, and the blush on her cheeks deepened, and her whole face began to glow—as if in that shout she had given voice to her life-long goal.

Bert bit his tongue.

He heard nothing.

Except Carla, who called out, "I'm starting to leak." With her free hand, she propped up her bosom.

Dramatic.

"We just had a baby," Bert apologized to the people at the neighboring table.

Congratulations.

"No, in the drawer above the eggs," Carla notified the home front.

"This is our first time out together," Bert continued to his neighbors. "Carla really needed a break."

The neighbors understood perfectly.

"Is everything going all right? When did she wake up?" Carla sounded jealous of the baby-sitter. "We'll be right home."

She hung up.

"Bert?"

That was the waitress's moment. She arrived with the coffees. Suddenly Bert couldn't keep his eyes off her navel.

"Bert? Shall we go?"

Carla's voice was one great yearning. For her child. For more children. Bert angrily straightened his glasses.

Translated by Manfred Wolf

Soft Landings

Remco Campert

> Of course, men have grown-up *moments,*
> a noble few scattered here and there,
> and of these, obviously death is the most
> important.
>> Truman Capote, *Answered Prayers*

ONE SUNDAY AFTERNOON in November the poet Onno Mulder took a walk through town. An extremely fine drizzle hung in the streets; he walked through the bottom of a cloud that could go no lower.

He liked this weather. Unlike sparkling sunshine, lashing rain, or biting cold, it made no demands on him, though it was far from characterless. It was weather that absorbed him without insistence.

As had happened frequently in recent months, his knee acted up a little when he got up, but the stiffness accompanied by a sickly pain vanished after an hour or two. This was another day when he felt no need to use the walking stick that he received last year as a joke from his friend Vollebracht on his fifty-eighth birthday.

He sometimes felt a sneaking urge to take the stick out with him anyway, so that they would be used to each other by the time even older age and its accompanying ailments appeared. But he was prevented from doing so by a slight feeling of embarrassment and by the thought that if he did it, he would have so much explaining to do to friends and other interested parties. Moreover, he was afraid that by using a walking stick he would write himself off for good as a suitor for the hand of young women, who he hoped would be impressed by his presence and not automatically dismiss him as "too old."

In fact it had been a diabolical gift, because the walking stick, which stood waiting in the hall by the hat stand until it was used, was a daily reminder to him of his future—or lack thereof. Since his birthday the phrase "old stick" had acquired its definitive meaning.

"Wear it out in good health," Vollebracht, who was the same age as he was, had said with a grin as he handed him the present. And Onno Mulder had grinned back as if they were sharing a secret.

Later in the evening they had taken turns hobbling around the room in the role of a comic graybeard, leaning heavily on the stick. With croaking voices they had harassed the other guests from the safety of pretended old age until Liza, Vollebracht's young new wife, had commented that "that was quite enough of that."

The object of his walk through town on this gray, damp afternoon was simply a walk. Nothing could be simpler, except that he had to choose his route carefully, because the town was strewn with bars, against whose attraction he had very little resistance. He was a periodic drinker, but the older he got the shorter the intervals between the periods became.

Every morning he resolved to leave alcohol alone at least for that day, but his thirst for booze would again win out for months on end and the consequences were becoming ever more apparent. Loss of memory, missed appointments, people whom he had supposedly insulted, and over and against this the incredibly charming way he engaged the company of complete strangers to whom he made promises late at night that he of course did not keep, since by the next day the events of the previous evening had been consigned to the ever-expanding realm of oblivion.

While he walked along the safe stretch of a canal (only farther along, across the bridge, there was a fatal pub that, as he knew from experience, never spat you out again until three in the morning), snatches of sentences surfaced in Onno Mulder's brain—word combinations that he tried out for a moment and then, when he found them wanting, abandoned again.

For over a year he had been writing a poem on the unexpected death of the man he had regarded as his best friend, the filmmaker Groenewei, who, after he had been diagnosed with a brain tumor, had turned in the course of a few months from a cheerful, eloquent chap into a dull-eyed, speechless wreck.

Since then not a day had gone by when Onno Mulder did not think of his friend; the sadness at his death would not recede.

In the beginning the poem had taken on the shape of his grief, a lament full of hand-wringing words and uncontrolled screeching flourishes. But he did not like the result of those outbursts of feeling; more than that, they awakened a kind of self-disgust: how was it possible that he, having practiced the art of poetry for all those years, could suddenly be converted to the amateurish view that sentiment, however honestly expressed, guaranteed quality?

In the middle of the night and under the influence of alcohol, Onno Mulder sometimes wrote furious letters to people whom, in his narrowing consciousness, he suspected of having inflicted or wishing to inflict harm on him. He saw through them; they mustn't think he was soft in the head. In his confused mind, the certainty that he was right seethed and raged.

Such attacks of berserk fury overcame him regularly, but he had learned not to go running to the mailbox in the middle of the night, but to let it rest until morning. So the next day he would find one of those angry epistles lying on the table: a silent, spattered witness of his intoxication. He would gather his courage and quickly read the letter through. Sometimes he did not even do that, but tore up the letter, with the feeling that he had escaped a great danger by the skin of his teeth. He couldn't afford to lose any more people from his life through his frantic behavior.

He did, though—albeit less and less—wonder what was wrong with him. When he had not been drinking he was mildness itself, a rather timid man who overlooked much that others did. When he drank way over the limit, he turned out to have a great reservoir of venom, which, once the tap was turned on, gushed unstoppably.

Even now that he was approaching sixty, Onno Mulder still had not finished raging.

Part of the problem was of course alcohol, but Christ, was he supposed to stop drinking? That would mean giving up the greater part of his social life. He could only really get on with people after he'd had a glass or two. Then he would start getting used to their presence and the feeling would grow in him that there was a point in talking to people and in them involving themselves with him.

And wherever you went, the drink was flowing, certainly in the town where he lived and in the circles he moved in. Still, he did not get the impression that everyone had the same affliction as he did. Some people kept themselves together easily without drink, while bottles were being emptied around them and new ones being brought. A long time ago, when smoking and drinking were still regarded as proofs of maturity, he had looked down a little on such people and also felt sorry for them: they didn't know what they were missing . . .

He regarded artists who were teetotalers with the same suspicion as he would members of a fanatic religious sect. They were dry as dust and did not dare to get to the bottom of things.

What did you know about life if you didn't sit in a late-night bar until six in the morning, in the noisy company of pimps, whores, burglars, painters, and chess masters? How could you ever gain an insight into human existence if you did not regularly go two nights without sleep, if you hadn't seen the glint of knives in badly lit alleys or listened to the tearful confessions of ex-SS-men far into the morning, if you hadn't slept in doorways or woken up on strange floors?

A poet must know the lower depths of life, so went his theory, which he had later unmasked as the umpteenth excuse for drinking.

Because what had actually come of all that knowledge of

the seamy side of life? A handful of poems (in the words of another Dutch poet) that projected the image of a young artist inclining toward romanticism. But there was a decisive element missing from that image: his own early death. Without that death all that black ecstasy was hard to take seriously.

Onno Mulder had simply gone on living, year in, year out. His poetry had changed and perhaps improved, but he had not been able to abandon his addiction to drink or the romanticism of destruction. It continued to dog him, an increasingly malevolent companion.

Before he reached the bridge, he turned promptly into a side street where there was no danger of facing a pub. Apart from a few houses it was lined with office blocks.

In one of those houses he had gone into hiding with some acquaintances when he had left his wife. He lived there with a temporary girlfriend. Constant inebriation helped him fool himself into thinking that he was crazy about this woman (who actually regarded him more as an interesting nuisance), and drink also helped him turn his feelings of guilt into a delusion of happiness.

He drew up great plans for a future life, free of all obligations and devoted to poetry, in another town in another country and probably also in another world. It did not take much effort for him to see his willful abandonment as the heroic epic of a man who, without counting the victims, remained true to his vocation. Perhaps he destroyed the lives of innocent bystanders, but after all he didn't spare himself either.

The girlfriend got fed up with it before he did and one

day upped and left. The weeks before she packed her things, they had rows every night and he would not rest until she threw something at his head in utter despair or burst into sobs or both.

Towering high above the world, without a soul to keep him company, he professed his poethood.

He held out all alone for a while in the attic that with great magnanimity had been placed at his disposal. When the last bars had closed he returned there, stumbled upstairs cursing, turned the radio on, and began wildly pounding at his typewriter.

With the talent for self-deception every lush has in abundance, he convinced himself that the gay couple putting him up were not inconvenienced by his presence. When he woke up in the silent house in the late afternoon he remembered virtually nothing of what had happened the previous day. Hence it was not difficult to opt for the idea that very little had happened and that this little had proceeded in comparative calm.

The couple were impeccable fellows with respectable jobs. One worked for a travel agency; the other was a civil servant at the town hall. Out of a kind of motherly concern they had taken him into their home, in the illusion that the example of their steady household would have a beneficial effect on his way of life, but the violence that was repeated every night finally became too much for them.

On a few occasions they summoned up courage and asked him if he could please be a little quieter; they didn't want to interfere with his life, but their house sometimes seemed like a late-night bar and that wasn't what they had in mind. With a guilty face and the disarming charm of the little boy caught red-handed, Onno Mulder promised to mend his ways. But that very same evening things would be just as bad again.

After the girlfriend had chosen the most sensible course of action, they cherished the hope for a little while that he would calm down, but that turned out not to be the case. Even by himself he made enough din for two people. So he had to leave; things couldn't continue like this.

Once they had made their decision they invited him for a bite to eat, because life was too short to part as enemies. While Onno Mulder approached the spaghetti bolognese without much appetite, they told him that they wanted to start using the loft themselves again and so, sorry old chum, but he would have to look for somewhere else to live.

It really didn't come as a shock. It hadn't been his intention for the situation to continue for as long as it had. Drinking and inertia had just stretched out his stay for so long that he had had the feeling he had always lived here and always would.

"When do you want me to leave?" he asked, bringing his wine glass to his mouth with both trembling hands.

The friends looked at each other to see if they had the guts.

One of them took a deep breath and said, "Tomorrow."

"We'd better be honest with you," said the other. "We don't need the loft immediately, but we'd like you to go tomorrow anyway. You're drunk the whole time and we can't take any more. We're awake half the night and that's not doing our relationship any good either."

"We're terribly worried about you," said one.

"Why are you destroying yourself? What on earth is the fun in that?" asked the other.

Onno Mulder, driven into a corner, shrugged his shoulders. How could he explain that his way of life was connected with his being a poet? At that moment, only halfway through his second glass of wine, it also struck him as a weak explanation. It would only gain force later in the evening.

"I'm sorry I'm so much trouble to you," he said humbly.

"And that dreadful girl," said one. "I hope I'm not insulting you, but she really was far beneath you."

"That's none of our business," said the other. "Have you got a place to go?"

"I'll find something," said Onno Mulder and in a gruesome vision saw the concourse of Centraal Station in front of him.

"Why don't you just go back to your wife?" asked one.

"It's not as simple as that," said Onno Mulder.

"It would be best if you first booked into a clinic to dry out," said the other.

"Perhaps that would be best," nodded Onno Mulder, his thoughts elsewhere, while he finished his glass of wine. He managed to bring the glass to his mouth with one hand and without spilling any. The poem would be called *Deportation*, a touch of Rimbaud, a touch of the Old Testament, and lots of himself and the modern world.

On this gray Sunday afternoon those events were long past, but not so thoroughly hidden from view by time that they didn't appear vividly to him again now as he was walking down the street. He looked up. Unlike before, the loft was almost all glass; an interior designer now had his studio there.

The gay couple had come to a sad end. One had died last year of AIDS and the other, shortly after burying his friend, had hanged himself. And I'm still walking around, thought Onno Mulder. It wasn't very fair, but it was reality, which in the case of the couple was almost kitsch, excessively pathetic—death had drowned itself out here in its effort to prove its point. Things could easily have been a bit calmer.

A couple of lines loomed up in his head, which faded and then, partially altered, returned. They were linked to images: a railway line, flat land, in the distance a mountain with its summit shrouded in clouds.

If he had somewhere to sit now he could write those lines down before they fled into the dark recesses of his mind.

While he tried to hold on to the words, he remembered how in the beginning the girlfriend he had lived with in the house of the gay couple had studiously written down the sentences inspired by alcohol that he produced at night in the certainty of being a great poet, effortlessly and without raising his voice. Convinced the following day that it could only be gobbledy-gook, he had always refused to look at it. She had (just in case) kept the sheets of paper in a folder, which she had taken with her when she broke free of his violence. Perhaps, he thought anxiously, they would turn up after his death and he would be unmasked as a basically talentless poet who was grossly overestimated in his day.

The side street issued into another canal. On the other side, the flickering neon logo of a fashionable bar beckoned—a green triangle, a yellow circle, and a couple of pink lines through them.

The poem in memory of his friend Groenewei would have to be a long poem, because only a long poem could do justice to the subject. And it must not be a lament, but (eureka! much better) an ode to life, because after all Groenewei had been a high-spirited man who, despite the many setbacks that were part and parcel of his profession, had never lost heart.

It had taken a tumor to do that.

And because death is already present at birth, Onno Mulder wondered if that tumor should be present from the first lines onward as a signal in the background—unrecognizable at first to the reader, who would only realize toward the end of the poem that death had always played a part in different disguises, the last of which it threw off at the end of the play.

The need to write something down mounted and, quickening his step, he walked down the canal, crossed a bridge, and went up the opposite side of the same canal until he reached the bar, which he entered without hesitating. He managed quickly to suppress the notion welling up in him that he was about to suffer the umpteenth defeat in his battle with drink. It was in the interest of his work that he was venturing into dangerous territory. Inspiration was now guiding his actions and it would turn against him if he hampered that process.

At this time in the afternoon it wasn't busy in the bar yet. There were some late risers leafing listlessly through papers, two young lovers holding hands silently across the table; and a young man with a floppy hat, which seemed one or two sizes too large, sat gazing out of the window after glancing at Onno Mulder.

Onno was not a regular visitor to this bar and the chance

of his meeting anyone he knew here was remote. He was the oldest person there, as was gradually becoming the case anywhere. For example, he hadn't been to the cinema for quite some time, because on the last few occasions he had been to a film he had the unpleasant feeling of having strayed into a kids' showing. His impression was that films were not being made for him anymore.

He asked the girl, who had left her place behind the bar and stood silently before him, for a cup of coffee. She was wearing black trousers, a white dress shirt, and a long white apron, like waiters in cabaret clubs in the last century. Her orange hair struck him as dyed, and on her nose she balanced a large pair of glasses with green frames. Perhaps he would pay more attention to her in a while, but for now his work took precedence.

As she walked back to the bar, he changed his mind and his order.

"No, no, just make that a tomato juice," he called after her. "With tabasco."

Whether it got through to her was not clear, since she didn't react.

He took his pen and a notebook that he always carried with him and wrote down the lines that had come to him. He wrote a few more that suggested each other as a logical sequence, but then his pen faltered. He read over what he had written and didn't think much of it at all.

What had seemed full of life and to the point when he was outside, made a faded, deficient impression once written down. Perhaps his brain had simply scrabbled those words together just to have an excuse for diving into a bar as soon as possible. How could he ever honor his friend

Groenewei if he went on writing this kind of limp, half-baked poetry? A poem on life and death and friendship must be powerful and compelling in its language; the writer must not create the impression for a moment that he had hesitated. Every line must seem to the reader inescapable and right on target, driven by a great breath and not a hesitant, fitful breeze.

Still silent, the girl set down a cup of coffee in front of him. He did not give rein to his sudden fury. As long as it wasn't alcohol it didn't really matter what he drank: it was all equally inadequate. A sharp longing for big glasses of beer rose up in him, and beyond that beer beckoned whisky, cognac, and gin, the safety of cigarette smoke and laughing pub friends.

Full of hatred, which at the same time struck him as ridiculous, he tore open the packet of sugar and emptied it into the insipid, dark-brown ooze. As he stirred the coffee and gradually felt his anger subsiding, he looked at the girl and wondered if she had heard him change his order. It might have been contrariness or perhaps she was one of those people so confused by unexpected changes that their brains refuse to register them, people who can only count to one, and then one again, and again. She was leaning with her elbows on the bar and reading a book—a peaceful scene (as if he were sitting at home and had a sister) that erased the last traces of his anger.

What book could she be reading? It probably wouldn't be poetry; or at least the chance of that was remote. One could say that in Holland there were more writers of poetry than readers, and it would scarcely be an exaggeration. Even the poets generally acknowledged as great sold poorly. It was only thanks to the stubbornness of a few publishers, a few critics, and of course the poets themselves that the genre still existed. Even in the bookshelves of his friends, for the most part people who did not eschew the written word, he rarely came across a collection of poems—unless they were themselves poets. Poetry was held in high regard, no one would dream of denying that, but few people felt called upon to read it.

Onno Mulder remembered the first time he had written something he was certain was a poem. At the time he was living in the woods with his family; it was summer, and he had just heard that his parents had decided to look for a house in the city and settle there for good.

Excited by the thought of the unknown future that awaited him, he had gone outside, into the woods he knew as well as his own room and the favorite books that were on the shelf of his foldaway bed. The sunlight slid through the canopy of leaves past the trunks of the trees onto the moss and his sandaled feet. Vague grief began sucking at his heart, as if he were already homesick for the landscape he had grown up with and through which he was still walking, but already a little as if he no longer belonged there. Nostalgia mixed with fear of what was to come: a life in the city, that mysterious enticing wonder, source of all energy.

When he got home hours later, he went straight to his room and wrote down something about the woods and the moss and his feet, the sound of the wood pigeon and the pounding of his bursting heart. He saw it was a poem when he'd finished it. He was a poet, his life had a purpose, he was ready for the city.

He had once worked on a script with Groenewei for a

television film about such moments of truth. For Groenewei it had been a Wayang puppet show that he had seen as
a boy in the Colonial Museum. They also talked to a com-
poser who stubbornly maintained that he had discovered
his vocation in the cradle when early one morning, even
before the first feeding of the new day, he had suddenly
noticed that the noise of his rattle was made up of different
sounds.

The script had disappeared into a drawer. They had realized fairly soon that such moments could not be put on the
screen. In fact they could only be told after the event, but
even then you missed the essence that was thoroughly lost
under subsequently added layers of views and explanations.

"So, Mr. Mulder, have you thought about it?" said a voice.

He looked up and saw the young man with the large
floppy hat standing by his table.

Onno Mulder had no idea what he meant.

"Er . . ." he hesitated, a receptive smile already creasing
his lips.

"André Berg," said the young man with the hat. "A couple of evenings ago we talked in the Hoek bar."

"Oh yes, of course," said Onno Mulder, as if the coin had
dropped, but he still didn't remember a thing. He did know
the Hoek bar. He wound up there only when he'd had a lot
to drink.

"Do you mind if I sit down for a moment?" asked André
Berg. "And can I get you a drink?"

"A toma . . . no, a tonic."

"Wouldn't you prefer something else?" said the young
man, who had sat down. "A whisky? I've got money now."

Onno Mulder shook his head. So he'd probably played Lord Bountiful in the Hoek bar.

"It was a fairly riotous evening, I think," he said, in an attempt to find out exactly what had happened that evening and what he was supposed to have thought about.

"It was great fun. And you helped my girlfriend a lot with what you said. She sees things completely differently now," said André Berg.

"I'm pleased to hear that," said Onno Mulder, relieved. Obviously he had been pretty smashed that evening.

"And that guy at the end, that wasn't your fault. He always kicks up a fuss when he's had a few."

"Oh yes, that's how it goes," said Onno Mulder. Why did the lad have a hat on? He remembered that at that age he had sported a beard for a while and always dressed in black.

He took a sip of his tonic and decided it would be best to come clean.

"You asked just now if I'd thought about it," he said. "But we talked about quite a few things, and I'm afraid I don't remember everything exactly."

"The poem," said André Berg. "The long poem you've written on the death of your best friend. You said you might publish it in our literary magazine. *Layers* . . . second issue. But you needed to think about it."

Onno Mulder bit his lip. Self-hatred swept over him. Drunkard's bluff and vanity had made him talk to complete strangers about a poem that wasn't even finished and that might never be finished if he went on like this. With the first stranger who came along he'd played the great poet who, despite his fame, was still a modest fellow and published his masterpiece in the anonymity of an obscure little magazine. He had squandered the friendship to ingratiate himself with a new generation. And what had he said to that girlfriend? If she were to come in now he wouldn't even recognize her.

"Perhaps I was a little premature," he said. "The poem is still far from how I'd like it to be."

André Berg looked disappointed. Probably he'd been bragging to his fellow editors. But like a good editor he persisted.

"Do you think you might be able to make it by the first of December? It ought to go into the Christmas issue, you see, and we'd like to give it plenty of publicity."

The Christmas issue of, what was it called again, *Layers!* Onno Mulder groaned inwardly. A literary magazine that still went in for a Christmas issue. What kind of world, scarcely one step removed from the school newspaper, had he blundered into?

"I'll do my best, but I can't promise anything," he said. "I have to go now."

He got up and quickly took his leave: the elderly poet who was entitled to his idiosyncrasies. He paid for his coffee at the bar and looked to see what book the girl with the orange hair and the glasses with green frames was reading. Gabriel García Márquez: *Chronicle of a Death Foretold.*

"Good writer," he said unsolicited as if to set his seal of approval on her reading. She smiled and nodded.

"Have you read it?" she asked.

"Of course," he said.

But that was another lie. His alcoholism had scarcely allowed him to read any books the last few years. During the few hours he still spent in a sober state he was too edgy to concentrate on a book; he derived his intellectual sustenance mainly from daily and weekly newspapers, so he could talk about almost anything, provided the conversation remained superficial, and it usually did. In this case there was the additional problem that the title of Márquez's book inspired fear in him. His instinct told him, rightly or wrongly, that giving himself over to a book with a title like that might demolish the barrier between him and his own death.

Outside it had turned a shade darker; the same haze still hung over the streets. The meeting with that young editor had disturbed his already fragile equilibrium; now he really wanted to dive into the first bar he came upon, but the predictability of the final result gave him just enough strength not to succumb to the temptation.

His mouth and lips were parched; his body on the other hand was soaked with sweat; the bittersweet taste of the tonic water was bubbling unpleasantly from his stomach. A group of Italian tourists in cheerful conversation came toward him, passed him, and their noise died away behind him.

He tried to think about the poem again, but, feeling insulted, it had retreated.

Mechanically he put one leg in front of the other without knowing exactly where he was walking or where he was headed. He felt completely empty. Only the weight of his shoes and damp clothes prevented him from floating away for good. The panicky idea that he was in danger of coming loose from the world brought Onno Mulder to a halt in front of what turned out to be the display window of a print-selling shop. He pressed his forehead against the glass.

An old etching of a canal had been given the place of honor in the middle of the window. After a while it dawned on him that it was a depiction of the canal he was on. This recognition brought him back to the reality of the moment and a little later he walked on until he reached a long shop-lined street, where he joined the flocks of strolling Sunday walkers.

In the city where he lived and in other towns he had visited and even in landscapes, there were spots that never let him down—and this street was one of them. They were safe havens that briefly relieved him from the anxieties and guilt that tormented him. They gave him the illusion of being in a world not controlled by phantoms.

Places for making a soft landing, Onno Mulder christened them in his own mind and, wherever he was, he was always searching for such places. He could never tell in advance where he would find one or what the place would look like. The fact that he felt at ease on this shop-lined street (it was more as if he had found his destination for a moment), did not mean that he had the same feeling on every shopping street everywhere in the world.

Cemeteries were places ideally suited to making soft landings; yet he knew of only one where that special peace descended on him: the cemetery of Montmartre in Paris, which was set like a little jewel inside the violence of the city.

The first time he went there was with Groenewei, who was looking for locations for a film about sadness, from which, of course, a cemetery could not be absent.

"No, this isn't it," Groenewei said after they had walked around for a while. "It's too . . . I don't know, I don't get any feeling here. It's not intense enough."

It was one of the few times that he felt an astonishment

bordering on irritation at the reaction of his friend, so strong indeed that he wondered for a moment if their friendship was not based on a misunderstanding, certainly when Groenewei turned out to prefer Père Lachaise, a pretentious necropolis that tried with hollow gestures to assert that something like immortality existed.

Groenewei's choice of cemetery, though, had not done the film any harm, since he won prizes with it at Oberhausen and Montreal.

The fact that he knew of more places for soft landings in urban areas than in the countryside was because the journeys he went on did not take him out of cities often or for very long. Also, when he found himself in the countryside, the need for such a spot was less great. Perhaps the countryside as a whole was a spot for making a soft landing. Although . . .

A year or so ago, after a drunken night, and filled with an unbridled longing to again see the woods that had been the cradle of his first poem, he took an early train. He got off in a provincial town and took a local bus, which after a drive along a new, unknown motorway, finally deposited him near the spot where he had spent his childhood—the primeval spot for making a soft landing.

The woods turned out to have been largely sacrificed. What was left of them was inaccessible. Bungalows had been built everywhere. Only here and there, in gardens where the closely mown lawn was king, did an original tree survive. The sandy path that had borne so many of his footprints had been widened and asphalted over. What had lived on in his memories as a wilderness, where only he knew the way, had become a neatly ordered residential area.

The house where his parents had lived was changed beyond recognition. A wing built largely of glass had been added, and it now housed a real estate office. At the side of the house, in the place where once there had been a rickety wooden shed—his headquarters—and from where he had embarked upon his campaigns into the surrounding area, a garage had sprung up. The front garden, once a mysterious, uneven area full of impenetrable bushes, had been leveled and supplied with the obviously compulsory lawn. There stood an empty flag pole waiting for a national holiday. On either side of what the current owner no doubt called "the driveway" (also paved), stood a lamppost, resplendent in the full glory of its degenerated beauty, a transplanted piece of the city's furniture.

It had obviously not been a good idea for Onno Mulder to return to his "roots." Cursing himself for his spontaneous impulsiveness—if he had been in a state in which he had been able to give it more thought, he would never have set out on this trip, even out of indolence—he walked back to the motorway just in time to catch the bus that came only every four hours.

This stroke of luck reconciled him somewhat with his failed mission, so by the time he got off at the provincial town, he was in quite a good mood. In a bar opposite the station he had an open-faced sandwich and drank a couple of beers. Feeling relaxed, he looked calmly at the billiard players and wished that he and the afternoon and the peaceful mood in the bar could go on forever. He started a poem that was intended to supplement the poem that once upon a far-gone time had come upon him in the woods. He ordered a gin and went for a long pee.

After a while, as quite often happened in bars, though he hadn't expected it here, someone spoke to him.

"Aren't you Onno Mulder?"

The man with the red face and the blond mustache who was called Van Rekum (at least that was the name that Onno Mulder heard), was a journalist at the local newspaper that appeared three times a week. He was also the correspondent for a national daily, but the news he passed on was seldom placed. And once, when a jet fighter had crashed into a farmhouse nearby, he happened to be on holiday.

"What brings you to this backwater?"

From the tone in which Van Rekum asked, one could deduce that he did not have a very high opinion of his hometown and that in fact he'd been born for something better.

"I spent my childhood here," replied Onno Mulder. It sounded like a reproach. "I have very happy memories of it."

Van Rekum went over to the bar and came back with two gins. After he sat down again, he said, "Perhaps it's a bit cheeky of me, but since you're here anyway, can I interview you? Then it can still make the Saturday edition."

"I can hardly refuse," said Onno Mulder.

One of the billiard players turned out to be the photographer of the local paper, and rather reluctantly interrupted his game to fetch his camera from home.

"It's my afternoon off, you know," said the photographer.

"This is news," replied Van Rekum, looking at Onno Mulder with a smile of understanding at such provincial obtuseness.

The interview took its course. Onno Mulder's form improved as more drinks were set in front of him. Poetry was scarcely mentioned, since Van Rekum, as he admitted honestly, was not that interested in it and was afraid that it would be over most readers' heads. Anyway, they were supplied with literary pieces by a press service they subscribed to.

What would interest readers was the newsworthy fact that he had grown up in this part of the country; the people could never get enough of news items about their own region. Onno Mulder said that his boyhood in this region had been of decisive importance for his writing and that the traces of it could still be found in his work, indeed that without the woods and the farms, the smell of manure and pickled turnips, and the prickly smell of wood smoke, he might never have written, at any rate not like he wrote now, and that people in the city had no idea of the value of the countryside and that more subtle joy and tragedy could be experienced on a single farm than in the whole greatly overrated city and that this was something most of his colleagues, against whom he would not say another word, had no idea of, imprisoned as they were in the smug notion that human life had found its most intelligent form in the city, while, he was bold enough to argue, more knowledge and feeling were involved in the sowing, tending, and finally uprooting of one feed beet than in, well you name it, anything at all in the city, which was hell on earth.

"But you people better watch things around here," he said to Van Rekum and to other figures who had moved their chairs closer as the afternoon progressed and who, so he thought, were listening in fascination to him, the poetic oracle from the big city. And he criticized in passionate terms the shameful way in which the woods of his childhood (his woods!) had been treated.

"Torenburg, the real estate agent," they all knew. Van

Rekum implied that he had information that showed this gentleman, who had a finger in every pie in town, in a very unfavorable light. But his editor in chief was thick as thieves with Torenburg, so I don't have to tell you any more about that, Onno.

Later the local lady bookseller also joined the group. He had been told about her—with lots of leering and winking and boyish nudging—before she came: she was a beautiful girl, a smashing girl, but sadly not interested in men. Onno soon got into a lively conversation with her about the plight of bookshops in a small provincial town. Poetry? If she sold ten volumes a year, that was a lot. The people around here were too level-headed for that; as if you had to be a frenzied muddlehead to read poems . . .

Still later a small group of them ate in a bistro that was "authentic French," with onion soup and French bread and a poster of the Eiffel Tower on the wall. Onno remembered snatches of this meal the following day, ghostly scenes from a silent movie: the wide, shocked eyes of Mrs. Van Rekum, summoned by her husband, when he had been unable to resist the temptation to force his hand between her knees under the table, the knocked-over wine glasses, his fall across the table as he got up to declaim a poem and also, oh shame, his wild screaming (the movie had not been that silent after all) in the direction of a table some way away where Torenburg, the real estate agent, was eating his *entrecôte provençale,* together with Van Rekum's boss.

The whole time he had felt himself a great poet, beyond all laws, far exalted above the demands of social propriety, a man who listened only to the call of the Muse.

His life seemed increasingly like a succession of such

scenes that took place in settings that were becoming more and more hackneyed.

As Onno Mulder made his way through the crowd along the shop-lined street, where people were looking in shop windows as far as lowered shutters allowed, the poem stirred diffidently into life again.

Dead friend—an opening that must be scrapped immediately—I evoke death in words. Station in a snowstorm, words that formed an image that he recognized as an experience he had shared with Groenewei. Time storm, it echoed in him. Words were fickle, unreliable; before you knew it they were leading you astray.

The image of a small station on the edge of a town, late at night, was clear—there was no way of changing any of that. Even if you tore up a photograph, because you could no longer bear the sight of what was depicted, the image still remained intact in your head.

Snow advanced from out of the darkness and, revealed by the light of the neon lamps on the station roof across the platform, was lost again, with a final glitter, in the darkness on the other side.

Why did such a still shot float to the surface?

Groenewei and Onno Mulder were standing on the platform, waiting for a train whose arrival was becoming more uncertain by the minute. For days, because of the merciless weather, the trains had been running at irregular intervals, and now it looked as if public transport had come to a complete standstill. The station was unmanned and the telephone box showed a vandalized handset, making it impossible to call for information.

"The world has come to an end, only we don't know," said Groenewei. He did not give the impression that it was distressing him. His look was cheerful and his small fat body, which scarcely came up to Onno Mulder's shoulders, exuded indomitability and enterprise.

"What shall we do? Shall we wait a bit or go back and find a hotel?"

"Let's wait ten more minutes," said Onno Mulder, who thought it not impossible that this enforced delay in icy wind and driving snow might eventually bear poetic fruit. The winter had a favorable effect on his creativity, he felt. Many expressions of lazy linguistic indulgence and the urge to embellish, were, as it were, nipped in the bud and killed.

He took another sip of cognac from the hip flask that he had put in his pocket earlier in the day just to be on the safe side. His friend, who was trying to get warm by beating himself with his arms, did not drink. Onno Mulder respected that with the protective love of the lush for the teetotaler.

They had spent the evening at an art movie house that featured on the program a number of Groenewei's shorts. The director had introduced his films and answered questions from the audience. Questions? One question about the precise dating of one of the films, and even that was asked by the manager of the art house, a hyper-nervous film freak with adolescent pimples and glasses covered in fingerprints that kept sliding off his nose.

Although Groenewei had a great reputation in avant-garde circles throughout the world, only eight people had shown up; no one had any problem blaming the poor turnout on the weather. The inevitable bar, which turned out to be a refuge for young people from the area, was fuller than the auditorium. During the showing of Groenewei's films the young people had to be asked to be quiet every so often. But Groenewei had a great evening, not only because he was a naturally sunny person, but especially because the manager had managed to get hold of Groenewei's first film, which had vanished without a trace years earlier at a festival in Montevideo, and whose maker had long since given up hope of ever seeing again. As payment, the manager gave Groenewei the copy he had found of his debut film.

The film was called *Happiness* and was only about four minutes long. In one continuous camera movement it documented the awakening and rising of a young girl (Groenewei's first girlfriend). The action took place in a garret (Groenewei's first room), the small window of which looked out onto a park, as could be seen when the camera (Groenewei's first camera) panned away from the girl for a moment and, after a short glimpse of the spring trees, rushed back to her and observed her stretching and yawning and smiling at the camera, throwing off the blankets, getting out of bed, hurriedly putting on a robe, and after some fiddling about with a cigarette and a lighter, leaving the room. She was followed by the camera into a narrow, dimly lit hallway until they both reached a sink where the girl, after studying her face in the mirror for a while, grabbed a tube of toothpaste and squeezed some of the white substance onto her toothbrush, which she brought to her mouth in close-up, and the film was over.

"Best thing I ever did!" cried Groenewei excitedly. "Isn't it touching? I'll never be that naive again. What did you think of it?"

"Sweet," said Onno Mulder. "Pristine."

"Pristine, yes, that's the word," nodded Groenewei, beaming. "A shot like that that never ends; I'd never dare do that anymore. You'd think it was terribly pretentious now. But it works here, don't you think?"

"Absolutely. It doesn't come across as dated at all. You can really only see that you made it a long time ago from her hairstyle and the brand of toothpaste. I don't think it exists anymore. Attractive girl, by the way. What happened to her?" said Onno Mulder, pleasantly tipsy.

"She's dead."

"Oh, I'm sorry."

"No, it doesn't matter. Once the film was finished, love was soon finished too. She wandered around Europe for a while with an American, a jazz musician, and died of an overdose in Barcelona. God, it's all a long time ago. Almost every film I make costs me a woman. Not that they all die, mind you. Eventually they do, of course."

How long ago was that evening? At least twelve years or so, Onno Mulder estimated. He hadn't known Groenewei so long then. He had met him when Groenewei had come up to him and asked him if he could use a poem of his as the basis of a film. That poem was best described as an attack of rage, at himself, at the world, come to think of it, at everything.

Groenewei's films always took an emotion as their theme: passion, grief, hatred, and now rage. They were hard to label. They were half documentary, half autobiographical— in earlier days his films would probably be called "film poems." Now they were difficult to pigeonhole, unless in the category "strongly personal expressions of a unique film talent that stubbornly goes its own way."

They had recognized something in one another and had immediately become friends, both with the feeling that the friendship had always existed. Onno Mulder had never got on so well with anyone. It was said that after forty it was difficult to make friends, so he had been lucky, especially if you remembered how many he had lost as a result of his unpredictable behavior.

The fact that he drank didn't bother Groenewei, nor did it bother him that Groenewei didn't drink. He did, though, exercise a degree of caution when he went out with Groenewei, so that the nightmarish aspects of his alcoholic's existence, of which Groenewei doubtless knew through other people's stories, did not rear their heads in his presence.

They could have grown old together, if Groenewei's fatal illness hadn't thrown a wrench in the works. And that was of course particularly unjust, since if anyone should have died it was Onno Mulder. But in that case too their friendship would have come to an end.

"Come, let's find a hotel. This is crazy," said Groenewei and a little later they were wading knee-deep through the snow in search of a hotel, which they had undoubtedly found, although at this moment, walking down the shop-lined street, Onno Mulder could not remember a thing about it.

Probably he had hung around the bar, while Groenewei, who took good care of himself, had gone to bed after placing his clothes neatly on hangers in the wardrobe and, on the low round table with the easy chair next to it, the can of film containing the black-and-white proof that his first sweetheart once existed.

The shopping street led into a square lined with bars, some with provocative neon signs on the front and the swinging and pounding of the latest pop music pouring out the door; others were darker, more veiled, with more muted lighting and a more staid clientele, brown pubs where an older poet could work on his poem in peace, his ode to life born of the death of his friend. Again Onno Mulder saw in front of him in a flash the station and the two friends bracing themselves against the wind: they would stand there forever in the hurtling snow.

Surely it must be possible, thought Onno Mulder as the craving for alcohol made his head swim, surely it must be possible for him, let's say for two or three weeks or so, every afternoon from, for example, two-thirty to five in a quiet pub like this where no one would disturb him and the waiter might have some respect for a drinking practitioner of the art of the written word, to work steadily on his poem until it was finished. And when his day's work was done, without things getting out of hand, for him to have another glass or two while listening with half an ear to the conversation of the regulars and the click of the billiard balls while he read the evening paper.

When he was young and badly housed and thought he had all the time in the world, Onno Mulder always wrote in bars. Not just poems, but also pieces for the newspaper and magazine stories, sometimes translations for the stage, all those things he did to keep himself and his poetry alive, were created there. He felt caught up in the tradition of, perhaps not the Dutch, but the European coffeehouse culture.

Drink had no part in it then, that came later, at night at parties, and served only to make his cheerfulness even more intense, the dancing wilder, and the lovemaking more impetuous. To drink at night, that was living poetically, pristinely, as pristinely as Groenewei's first film, the beautiful face that in the morning light, after briefly blinking, burgeoned brightly, the lips that curled up in the corners of the mouth, the light that timelessly stroked the hand that brushed the hair away.

But gradually this bright beginning had become murky and misguided in an increasingly dismal decline. The spontaneous joy and urge to discover with which he had once abandoned himself to poetry had gradually degenerated into punitive exercises in self-discipline. His poetry was a tattered flag, though he still wouldn't lower it.

Wedged between two bars was a sandwich shop; Onno Mulder went in. He ordered a roll with steak tartare and chopped onions.

"Do you have any beer?" he asked.

"No, we don't sell beer. You'll need to go next door for that."

"A buttermilk then."

Of course he knew they didn't sell beer, yet he couldn't help asking for some. And it was as if uttering the word "beer" liberated him. Even though he had negotiated a short delay by asking for a drink in this of all places, it would only be a little while before the first glass of the day was in front of him. He had made his decision and felt his somber mood receding, giving way to excited expectancy and even zest for work.

It was not inconceivable that, if he set his mind to it now he could write down the Groenewei poem in one go, relieved as he was of his drinking problem. Too much energy was wrapped up in struggling with that, energy that he needed all too badly for the poem and hence must no longer waste.

Onno Mulder regarded the Museum of Modern Art in Amsterdam, of which he had been a regular visitor since he had moved there, as one of the places for making a soft landing. For years he went there only for the art, which couldn't be modern enough for him and gave him the feeling, in this part of the world that was not so sensitive to art, that he nevertheless belonged to an international brotherhood of art, whose avant-garde manifested itself not only in New York and a few other cities where people were rolling in money and love of art, but in this city too.

His interest (oh, why not call it love?) for what painters did had not diminished over the years, and he still visited the museum often, although he no longer went to every exhibition. But the very knowledge that all those works of art were hanging there, all those fruits of the endeavors of dedicated titans, gave Onno Mulder a sense of belonging. In this world he felt at home and in this building he felt safe. He too had contributed to the wear on the marble steps that led to the upper floor, except perhaps in the period when he wore sneakers that were all the rage then.

Sometimes he could not suppress a slight feeling of jealousy when he noticed how many people (sometimes whole families) were so obviously attracted to his contemporaries who were painters. Undeniably poets had missed the boat somewhere.

Before he set out for the museum, he drank a second glass of buttermilk in the sandwich shop: it could do no harm now that the decision had been made. In the philanthropic mood that had come over him now that he had decided on the course of the rest of the day to a certain extent, he even entered into a brief conversation with the gray-haired gentleman who made the sandwiches about the annual increase in the number of tourists in the town—particularly Italians, it had struck him.

"You won't hear me complaining, sir."

"No, I can imagine. Right, I hope business stays good," said the poet and, as a man of the world, left slightly too small a tip.

With a determined gait he walked in the direction of the museum. The weather was still the same and the light was almost evening light, although it wasn't even four o'clock yet.

As he walked down the wide street lined with tall trees on which the museum was located, he stopped for a moment, as was his wont, in front of one of the houses and looked closely at a spot on the front. Yes, the four crosses scratched in the gray stone were still there, and there was a good chance that they would still be there long after he was dead and buried and his poems had been forgotten.

Before he continued on his way he ran his forefinger over the scratches. He had made them on the front of the house long ago with the point of the pocket knife that he always carried with him in those days as a reminder of his boyhood in the woods.

Each cross stood for each time he went to bed with his girlfriend Myra, who lived with her aunt and was in the first year at drama school. Late at night, when the aunt was fast asleep, he crept upstairs to Myra.

Their love had lasted no longer than four crosses. He did not know what had become of Myra; at any rate she had not become a famous actress. His memory of her was vague; she had slightly Native American features and sometimes she would suddenly burst into tears, without him being able to figure out why. But he still vividly remembered the feeling he had early in the morning, with auntie still fast asleep, when he left the house after sleeping with Myra for the first time, or rather, sleeping with a woman for the first time. It had been a feeling of great triumph. The world was his oyster; no harm could befall him. The world would hear more of him.

Fate smiled on Onno Mulder in the museum. He hurried to the restaurant without further ado and as he shuffled forward in the self-service line, he saw that the people sitting at his favorite table in the corner at the back were preparing to leave. A few reluctant children still had to be hoisted into heavy jackets.

By the time he had paid for his bottle of wine (he decided against beer at the last moment—too cold) the table was free, but other people were on their way to it. He strode behind them, passed them at the last moment, and quickly sat down. After some grumbling, the others slunk off.

He laid out everything on the table in preparation—notebook, pen, cigarettes, lighter—then unscrewed the bottle of wine and filled his glass. He drank it in two gulps and refilled it. He lit a cigarette, picked up his pen, stared at the paper, but not a word came. *Death*, he muttered under his breath, *life*, in the hope that saying these words would trigger a chain reaction.

When this failed to happen, he took another gulp and let his eyes wander around the restaurant, looking pensive, in case anyone was watching him. Near the entrance to the restaurant, among the busy throng of people leaving and others taking their places, he saw his friend Vollebracht standing with Liza, his new young wife. They were looking around for a place. Onno Mulder stood up and waved to them, until they saw him and their faces lit up.

"Can we join you for a bit or are you busy?" asked Vollebracht, pointing to the pen and the notebook.

"No, come and sit down. I was just finishing," said Onno Mulder. "That's it for today."

"I'll get something to drink," said Liza. "Something for you too?"

"Bring some more wine for me," said the poet.

"Do you often work here?" asked Vollebracht. "Isn't it far too busy here?"

"That's exactly what I like about it. Then I feel as if I'm still participating in life, to some extent."

"How weird seeing you here," said Liza, who had returned with a full tray. "I dreamt about you last night. Isn't that crazy? I normally never think of you."

"Now, now," said Vollebracht.

"I don't mean it like that. You understand what I mean."

"Of course," said Onno Mulder. "What did you dream then?"

"I was on top of a mountain and it was pretty scary, because there were clouds all around me, and I didn't dare take a step. And at the same time, the way that can happen in dreams, I saw you down below in the distance and I thought, it's safe there, and I called to you, but you didn't hear me. In any case, you just kept on walking. A little later I was in a train, but that's already another part of the dream. Odd, isn't it?"

Vollebracht looked put out.

"I doubt if it's so safe with him," he said.

"It was only a dream," said Liza.

"You won't believe me, but I know that dream," said Onno Mulder. "This afternoon I was walking through town and I suddenly saw the image of a mountain with clouds around the summit and I was walking across a plain and there were railroad tracks, but no train."

"You're making it up," said Liza incredulously.

"I swear to you I'm not. Are you sure you never think of me?"

"Yes. But perhaps you sometimes think of me."

"Just try all the people who think of mountains at this time of year with the skiing holidays just ahead," grumbled Vollebracht, who felt that things had gone quite far enough. "Pure coincidence. Please spare me the wishy-washy theorizing."

"A person's allowed to dream, isn't he?" said Onno, winking at Liza.

"Oh, the old man gets upset so easily," said Liza.

When the museum closed its doors, all three of them thought it would be a good idea to go for a drink somewhere.

On the cusp of Sunday night and Monday morning, Onno Mulder woke up in a corner of the doorway of his house.

He was sitting slumped over on the cold, hard stone. He saw in the light of the lamppost outside his house that his house key lay beside him. He reached up, took hold of the door handle, and with great difficulty hoisted himself up. Pain shot through his knee.

Once he was inside and had closed the door, his heart was pounding and his blood was pulsing so wildly that he felt faint and soon sank onto the bottom step of the stairs that rose above him like the ascent to yawning nothingness.

He sat like that for a while, dizzy and shivering with cold.

Surely I'm not going to die now, it flashed through him. I can't, I've still got that poem to write.

Onno Mulder got up and maneuvered himself upstairs, holding on to the banisters with both hands.

Translated by Paul Vincent

A Pounding Heart

Marion Bloem

THE CITY WAS MY AUNT'S WORLD; the small town
was my home. My mother was strict, and my aunt Sissy let
you do anything. My mother had all the physical charac-
teristics of an Asian woman, because she resembled her
Indonesian grandmother. My aunt, however, was blond
with green eyes, pale skin that couldn't take the sun, and the
classic features of her European grandfather. Only when
they laughed could you see that they were sisters, because
then they spoke the same physical language.

There were other differences. My aunt disliked cooking,
and my mother was considered a kitchen goddess. My
mother had polio when she was young, and as a result
lacked the expected symmetry that belongs to the human
body.

My aunt, on the other hand, had a body like that of the
movie stars she idolized. Her walls were covered with photographs of Greta Garbo, Doris Day, Romy Schneider, and
Marilyn Monroe, as well as the members of the Dutch
Royal House. On my mother's walls hung Balinese wood-
cuts, Sundanese masks, Jogjakartan silver, Javanese *wajang*
puppets, and a Sumatran *kris*, all brought from Indonesia,
her country of birth and that of her sister.

During summer vacations, my cousins stayed with us. The wooded surroundings were supposed to give their pale faces some color. And if my aunt was once again bothered by her gallstones, the boys would be sent to my mother's and go to our school for a while.

Christmas vacations, fall vacations, and spring vacations, as well as weekends, on the other hand, my sister and I spent at my Aunt Sissy's in Amsterdam. Usually my mother was there as well, and then it was as if she had brought along the monotony and boredom of our little town in our suitcase. Her watchful eye restricted our fun on Sunday afternoons after church until, encouraged by Aunt Sissy, she would allow us to go with our cousins to the parochial cinema where Laurel and Hardy movies were shown for a nickel a person.

After my aunt was forever relieved of her gallbladder troubles, thanks to an operation, and once we had a little brother, my mother would return with the baby to the little town after bringing us to the capital by train. Only then were my sister and I able to discover the big city.

Aunt Sissy lived at the edge of the Jordaan, the oldest part of the city, referred to by many as the Heart of Amsterdam. She rented a tiny flat above a barbershop on Marnixstraat.

The barber, with his gray, pomaded head shaved close on the sides and back, who looked like a man but moved like a lady, spoke with a Jordaan accent that was already fascinating in itself. We had to enter on tiptoe, sneak up the stairs, and whisper, or else the barber, who was also the owner of the building, would get angry.

There was only one way to get my aunt angry: by annoying the barber. Then she would grab her slipper and run after her boys with it. And if she didn't manage to catch them, she would throw both slippers at them, then anything else she could lay her hands on, until one of the boys was hit and would start to cry.

Her aim wasn't very good, so the pursuit would stir up a racket that made the barber furious. He would storm up the stairs and pound on the door until my aunt opened up. My cousins would be as quiet as mice for the rest of the day, anxious about the moment my uncle, who was in the navy, would come home. Whether he came back that same evening or two months later, they could count on a spanking if the barber had come to the door. I still don't know whether it was Aunt Sissy or the barber himself who would tell my uncle.

The barber never complained about all the noise when these severe corporal punishments were dealt out—as if he took pleasure in hearing my uncle carrying on like that, or were afraid that he would be hit as well if he banged on the door for silence.

I hated the barber and blamed him whenever my uncle punished my cousins. I would peer into the barber's shop to give him a dirty look, my heart in my throat because we were forbidden to spy on him. The barber did not want to be reminded in any way that he shared his house with children.

A lot was forbidden, but a lot more was possible at my aunt's. Playing soccer in the street wasn't allowed. It was hardly possible anyway because a tram ran down the busy Marnixstraat thoroughfare. It kept me awake at night particularly because of the bridge it had to cross after passing the house. First came the loud ripping clang of the tram bell, with which the conductor gave warning that the tram was rounding the corner, and then: kabonk, kabonk, kabonk, kabonk, kabonk.

As soon as the tram went over the bridge, it seemed as if the heart of the city were beating with fear, and my own heart rate would adapt, as if automatically.

I would hear the breathing of my two cousins in the upper bunk, and the regular breathing of my sister, who shared the lower bunk with me. How was she able to sleep so peacefully when the city was so restless?

It was a brick, three-story corner building with thin walls. Whenever the tram sped up to make it over the bridge, it sounded as if it were running straight through the wall. My mother said that an earthquake in Indonesia made their house shake the way a passing tram did in Amsterdam.

Now, forty years later, the building is still there, and it is even smaller than I recall. A very narrow, steep staircase led up to the apartment. You entered through a small living room that my uncle, the few times he was home, half filled all by himself. In three steps you were at the window that looked out on the street, the tram tracks, and an alley. Another step to the right landed you in the boys' room. From that window you could see the bridge over the Brouwersgracht.

The boys' bedroom had a bunk bed in it, and hardly any place to walk. Their boxes of toys were tucked under the bed. With a little limberness you could pull them out, shove them in the direction of the living room, and then tip them out so that the little cars, soldiers, and Lego pieces tumbled across the thin sisal carpet.

The living room was chock full, as were many of the Jordaan living rooms I glanced into out of curiosity when I walked down the streets. My aunt collected plush stuffed animals, kitsch porcelain figurines, dolls in traditional costume, and mounted animals that my uncle had brought back from all his distant voyages. As for playing, there wasn't much room. The empty toy boxes would block our view of the living room when we rolled our Matchbox cars and Dinky toys alongside and underneath the bunk bed.

In the wall across from the window—the partition between the boys' room and the stairway landing—was a door that was blocked by the bunk bed. I was bewitched by that door, and at night would fantasize about it opening and the bunk bed being pushed out the window by the force of the door swinging open.

Through the chinks I could see when the light in the stairwell went on, and if I squinted hard through the crack, I could see whether it was the barber or his elderly mother trudging up the stairs.

The walls in the boys' room were covered with taped-up pictures of movie stars, because whenever the boys couldn't get to sleep, they would pick at the wallpaper, peeling off more each time. My cousins treated the actresses, with their provocative, low-cut necklines, with more respect than they did the original flowered wallpaper.

The walls seemed made of cardboard. When I knocked on them it sounded much the same as when I knocked on an empty toy box. I couldn't knock on some areas without hurting my knuckles though, while in other places I could hear the grit fall. The nights lasted a long time in that little room. . . .

To get to the toilet at night, I had to go through the living room with all the mounted animals that looked as if they were reproaching me for having been killed and then stuffed with cotton balls. The turning lamp with colored bulbs created moving shadows on the wallpaper.

Through the living room I would come to a narrow passageway where my aunt had made a place for her youngest son to sleep. And after that I would be in my aunt and uncle's bedroom, which was dark enough during the day, but pitch black at night. A scent hung in the air there that I have never smelled anywhere else.

To the left in that dark space was a passageway that led past a small kitchen—with just enough room for one person—and ended straight ahead in a tiny room with a toilet. As in most of the old houses in the Jordaan, they didn't have a full bathroom. We had to clamber up on the counter to wash ourselves in the kitchen sink. Sometimes my aunt filled a basin in which we were allowed to take turns washing. When we stepped out, we left puddles behind on the sisal carpet, which would quickly be wiped up by Aunt Sissy. "The floor is thin," she would say. "Otherwise the water will drip down on the heads of the barber's clients."

Across the street from the building there was a narrow alley, and this is where the boys would play soccer if Aunt Sissy didn't have supper ready yet. It was a good thing they got a lot of pocket money from their father. Since their ball would be taken away by the alley residents on an average of three times a week, the boys spent most of their pocket money on rubber balls.

My cousins excelled at soccer, and for that reason, despite their bad reputations, they had not yet been kicked out of school. Without them, the school would have made a pitiful showing against the other school teams in the city. But

even for my talented cousins it was difficult to use the wall
as a goal, without hitting one of the windows when they
tried to score.

There was no neighborhood square to play in, the sidewalk was narrow, and although children might have been
generally well liked in that part of the Jordaan, my cousins
certainly weren't in this particular neighborhood.

My sister and I, typical small-town girls, worshiped by
neighbors and teachers alike because we were the only colored folk in a white town, were good. We did our homework conscientiously and were the best students in our
class. My cousins, however, got nothing but failing grades,
and were already skipping school at an early age. They said
that the house was too small for doing homework. My aunt
seemed to accept that explanation, or else she didn't want
them around the house too much on account of the slightly
dotty barber, because my cousins were sent to the park on
days when they had no school, as well as after school.

As soon as we had breakfast under our belts, we had to
go to Westerpark, the park right near the old west-end gas
plant, with two cookie tins filled with sandwiches. My
cousin got the house key placed around his neck, and we
had to promise not to come home before six o'clock. She
would give us extra money to buy ourselves treats, while my
mother forbade snacking on sweet things and thought one
cookie a day was more than enough.

Aunt Sissy would go to the matinee with a girlfriend, or
comb through all the stores with clothing on sale. Not only
did she have an extensive wardrobe, but my cousins did as
well. They went to school in bow ties and plaid suits.

We didn't tell my mother—who was furious if we came

home not at five o'clock, but at five past five—that Aunt Sissy preferred us to stay out as long as possible. In a twinkling we would empty our plates of Dutch mashed potatoes and greens, and be sent straight to bed. Brushing our teeth didn't seem to be important. Aunt Sissy saw this as an attempt to delay bedtime.

When my uncle was home we were allowed to stay up late. At around eleven o'clock at night he would send us off to get Italian ice cream or snacks on Haarlemmerplein. Then we would also take a little stroll along the canals. My cousins would try all the doors to the stores in case somebody had forgotten to lock up. They looked for bicycles that weren't locked. I would walk apprehensively behind them, afraid that we were staying out too long and that my uncle was going to let them have it.

My cousins went into giggling fits whenever I let on about my uneasiness. "My dad's only too happy if we're out of the way," said my oldest cousin. I had no idea what he meant, but concluded from his knowing little wink that it would be better to act as if I understood him.

We revealed very little to my mother about our stays at her older sister's. She was allowed to know that before we went to church on Sundays, Aunt Sissy combed our hair for hours and tried all kinds of styles, and that on Saturday nights she put prickly curlers in my hair, making it impossible for me to sleep at all.

We did recount in great detail what she had cooked all those days. My mother would react by vehemently shaking her head. "Why doesn't she cook rice?" How could her sister be so lazy! Dutch food wasn't healthy fare in my mother's eyes; it was a way for a housewife to get off easy.

The nights in Amsterdam are what I remember most vividly from my childhood. When the trams stopped running, the shouting on the street would start. Across from the building was a bar, and there was always a scene going on outside. Usually it was a woman who would yell as she roused her drunk husband out of the bar with a rolling pin, letting him have it out on the street.

I had seen cartoons in magazines that showed women with rolling pins waiting for their husbands behind doors, and found it incredibly fascinating that I was able to observe this firsthand. I can still feel the throbbing under my tonsils, as if my heart had taken the elevator up and gotten stuck in my throat. My mother didn't have a rolling pin: she rolled out her dough with a bottle. And my father drank no alcohol and had never set foot inside a bar.

We didn't go just to Westerpark. After an hour or so my cousins would get bored. In the park my cousins felt less inclined to play soccer, as if all the excitement went out of scoring a goal if there weren't any windows in the balance. My sister and I would follow them to the beltway of canals downtown.

We would watch with shame as they jumped from houseboat to houseboat, and pushed bicycles into the canals. Proudly they would count up the bicycles they had tossed into the water in a single day. The tally was kept in ballpoint lines on the palms of their hands. They would keep track of their records in their school notebooks at home.

They would egg us on to step onto a houseboat, too, walk on the roof of a boat, or push a bicycle over the side. But my heart would already be beating hard enough just from

looking at their bad-boy pranks. Not a bone in my body
dreamed of imitating their bad-boy behavior.

But the excitement that they aroused in me, the running
out of breath whenever we had to make a dash for it and hide
somewhere because a grown-up was on our heels, did me
good. It was as if the blood flowed faster through my veins
if I skipped along after them down the canal streets. This
was the city at its best. In Amsterdam I learned that the
harder you let your heart pound, the more fun life becomes.

I had more of a problem with their daily raids along
Haarlemmerdijk. They stole everything they could lay their
hands on, purely and simply for the thrill of it. And my sister and I had to stand guard or distract the person tending
the store so that they could carry on.

I didn't want to leave my cousins high and dry, but I didn't
enjoy this complicity one bit. For that reason I still avoid
Haarlemmerdijk. I can't walk there without feeling guilty.

My grandma lived in West Amsterdam. The ride on the
L bus to Grandma's was a fun, safe excursion. My cousins
wouldn't go straight to her apartment on Schaapherder-
straat, since they first wanted to do a little shoplifting at the
V&D department store across from the old church, referred
to as the Coal Bin. We were supposed to keep an eye out
for men in trench coats who might be walking around,
while my cousins hid cellophane packets of postmarked
foreign stamps under their blazers. With the staplers, rubber stamps, and other office supplies they had stolen on
Haarlemmerdijk, we would play post office in the portico
of my grandma's building.

I would secure stamp booklets and gift certificates from

the supermarket, which wasn't really stealing since they were available for free. But I still felt pretty tough when I ran out of the store with a whole pile. Despite the legality of the action, I would glow with excitement, and just like my cousins I would get to my grandma's with rosy cheeks.

Grandma would take us on tram number 13 to Cineac, the movie theater downtown that showed musicals starring Elvis or Cliff Richard. We would wait in line for a long time in the rain, and she would send my cousins out to buy french fries and croquettes. My sister and I had to stay and wait beside her in the rain. She was afraid that something would happen to us because we were girls and because we weren't city kids.

It wasn't without envy that I would listen to my cousins' panting when they sanctimoniously handed over the pointy little paper sacks. "Have you been up to some kind of mischief?" Grandma would ask sternly. Vigorously their heads shook no, but it was as if the beating of their guilty hearts drowned out the trams.

When my aunt moved to a small suburb outside the city, I missed it. My cousins live with their proper little families in small towns and don't miss the city. They say that theirs was an unhappy childhood, and they don't go to Amsterdam any more, even to catch a movie.

But I bought a house in the Jordaan. I can't live any longer without a pounding heart.

Translated by Wanda Boeke

Living in the Red-Light District
Maarten 't Hart

IN 1956, WHEN ASKED in an interview what the best environment for a writer was, William Faulkner replied, ". . . The best job that was ever offered to me was to become a landlord in a brothel. In my opinion it's the perfect milieu for an artist to work in. It gives him perfect economic freedom; he's free of fear and hunger; he has a roof over his head and nothing whatever to do except keep a few simple accounts and to go once every month and pay off the local police. The place is quiet during the morning hours, which is the best time of the day to work."

For a Dutch writer, however, it's not easy to take up residence in a whorehouse. Country brothels don't usually rent out rooms as living quarters to private individuals, and in cities like Amsterdam and The Hague there is such a shortage of housing that writers, whose work does not generally tie them to a city, would not be given residence permits for a pied-à-terre above a brothel. In the Netherlands the closest thing to Faulkner's ideal is to settle in a red-light district. And so, in the year of Our Lord 1980, I followed in the footsteps of many other writers and artists and bought a house that had been declared a historic monument on Oudezijds Voorburgwal in Amsterdam. I intended to rent out most of the old, narrow seven-story house to friends of mine who had already spent years searching desperately for a place to live, and I wanted to keep one room for myself, to stay in regularly and write.

The first time I spent a few days there, in the summer of 1980, I decided to find out how much it would cost to do what I liked doing best. Making my way between sauntering men and whispering women, I walked from my house across the bridge to the square by the Old Church. How much, I wondered. I knew how much it usually cost in other cities, but would they charge the same in Amsterdam? At the entrance to the Old Church I met a young woman who said, "I have no idea if it's possible or what it would cost, but you could phone and ask." She gave me a telephone number, and I walked back to my house. I dialed the number and heard a deep male voice on the other end of the line.

"Sir," he said, "you can't play it just like that. First you have to prove your skills."

"Gladly," I said.

"Fine," he said, "then come tomorrow morning at nine and show us what you can do. If you're good enough, you can have a go, and in that case it will cost fifty guilders an hour."

I was so surprised I didn't answer right away. Fifty guilders an hour! I'd never had to pay that much anywhere. It was exorbitant, but I wanted so badly to play that organ, at least once. I promised I'd be there the next morning at nine.

"Don't forget the fifty guilders," said the man.

After that conversation I went outside again. I walked through narrow streets where love was being offered for money despite the early hour, and soon reached Nieuwmarkt. Next to the Weigh-House I saw a man selling fruits and vegetables. Lying in small crates were all kinds of large, exotic fruits. Surrounded by papayas and pomegranates was a large, prickly monster of a fruit. Was it a durian? Was it for sale? I knew, of course, that it gave off an unbearable stench when you cut into it. No problem there: I could cut open the durian in the cellar and carry the creamy flesh of the fruit upstairs to my room.

"May I have the durian?" I asked the vendor, who was eyeing me suspiciously.

"Yes," he replied curtly, "you're in luck, it's good and ripe."

The man was about to put the durian in a paper bag when I said, "Don't bother, I can put it in my own bag."

"Right, sir," he said, "that will be fifty guilders."

Fifty guilders! For one piece of fruit! I wasn't even sure I had that much money on me.

"Sure is expensive," I said guardedly.

"Not at all, sir," he said, "it comes by plane from Indonesia, saves you the trip."

I gave him all the money I had, and took my durian home to my cellar. In a narrow lane that, considering the neighborhood, bore the appropriate name of Monnikenstraat— Monks Street—someone was tapping loudly on a windowpane. I turned around and looked. A dark-haired girl wearing a low-cut blouse and gold bikini bottoms was motioning to me to come inside. My only thought, of course, was that she was inviting me in for a paid visit to her purple-lit room. Calmly, I shook my head and walked on down the street, but soon I heard the clicking of heels behind me. Someone grabbed my arm and I looked around.

"May I ask you something?" It was the girl in the gold bikini. I detected a slight German accent.

"Of course," I said.

"Then come with me," she said.

What was this all about? Once inside, improper pecuniary propositions would no doubt be forthcoming. She saw me hesitate, apparently realized what I was thinking, and said, "No, no, it's not that, just come with me."

I followed her to her small purple-lit room. Six torn-open condom wrappers were lying in an ashtray. A bath towel was spread out on the bed.

"I heard you bought a house here," she said.

"Who told you that?" I asked, surprised.

"My neighbors," she said, "and they heard it from your next-door neighbors. Here everybody knows everything about everyone. But what I wanted to ask you was if I could rent an apartment in your house?"

"I've already rented out the whole house," I said, dumbfounded, "at least I think I have . . ."

"There isn't even an attic room left?"

"Well, there's a translator who still hasn't made up her mind whether she wants to move in or not."

"If she doesn't, then could I . . ."

"I don't know," I said.

"How much would it cost? What are the others paying?"

"The man renting the upstairs apartment will be paying 350 guilders a month, the woman downstairs 400 a month."

"Isn't that a bit underexaggerated? I'd be prepared to pay you a lot more, as long as I can pay cash."

Underexaggerated, I thought, how funny! We don't have a word for that in our language, and here she's supplied it

95

effortlessly. Just because of that wonderful word, I said, "Well, if the translator doesn't come, I'll keep you in mind."

"Oh, that's nice of you. Would you like a cup of coffee?"

She'd already made coffee, and poured me a cup, putting it next to the ashtray with the condom wrappers. Pointing at the wrappers, I asked cautiously, "What does it cost, actually?"

"A trick?" she asked. "Fifty guilders for a straight lay, but most men, well, they want it with soapsuds."

Good God, I thought, everything here costs fifty guilders. The trade unions must be behind it, bringing prices in line with each other. A durian, a lay, playing the organ for an hour in the Oude Kerk—it all costs fifty guilders. I was about to ask: With soapsuds? How does that go? when she said, "I'm living in a bad neighborhood and I'd really like to get out. I'd love to rent an apartment around here, or buy it if necessary. In the long run I'd like to open up a café."

"And stop doing this?" I asked, pointing at the condom wrappers.

"Yeah," she said, "it's not exactly my hobby, you know."

"How did you end up here, then?" I asked.

"I came here on vacation from Austria, and I thought to myself, I have to move here, this is perfect, I could really make some money. So I went back to Austria, got everything settled, and came back here as fast as I could."

"But couldn't you do this there?"

"Not like I can here. I liked the atmosphere here, I still do. It's fun, and the people are nice. I only work in the morning, when it's still quiet, and even then I get enough customers. Now I have to get back to work, though. Will you think of me if something becomes available in your house?"

On the way home to my cellar that curious comment kept running through my head. "Most men want it with soapsuds." How on earth could I find out what that meant? One way was to get some money, go back to her, and say, "I'd also like it with soapsuds." Then what? Would I be allowed to blow purple bubbles at her gold bikini?

Several years have passed, and I still don't know what it means to do it "with soapsuds," but I'm grateful to her for introducing me to life in the red-light district with that remark. Just after the war, my mother used to hoard Sunlight soap, stowing away boxes and boxes of it under my bed, so that I always fell asleep with the penetrating smell of soap in the air. At night I dreamed of foamy water and I often woke up from a terrible nightmare, convinced my eyes were full of soap. So it's hardly surprising that five years or more of Sunlight sleep managed to instill in me a lifelong aversion to soap. The words "with soapsuds" endowed me with an instant and amazingly effective immunity to the temptations of the red-light district. They did it with soapsuds. Yuck!

That ominous reference to soap enabled me, for as long as I had my room there on the third floor, to observe the colorful activity all round me with a certain sense of detachment. The fact that I'm a morning person is an added bonus, though I'm afraid Oscar Wilde once said of people like me, "Only dull people are bright at breakfast." From the crack of dawn until the mid-morning coffee break—the best part of my day—the red-light district is the very picture of peace and quiet. There are hardly any cars. What you do see at this hour in many of the still-lit rooms are the bent backs of women in sleeveless aprons, performing their cleaning operations with grim determination. Everywhere there are vacuum cleaners droning, dustcloths flapping, and machines busily polishing the tiled floors. In many apartments the rooms in question are even hosed down, as though they're trying to wash away years of dirt. If you take a walk at six in the morning you imagine yourself to be in a past century, when maidservants still scrubbed the cobblestones every day. All the same, it seems like an inordinate amount of housework. Why do those rooms have to be cleaned so thoroughly? Do they have to erase every last trace?

After everything has been cleaned in the early hours, a strange, pure, peaceful atmosphere settles over the neighborhood. If you take a walk at this time you think you're in a deserted part of town full of forgotten canals. You could easily go home and write, "The place is quiet in the morning, which is the best time of day to work." As soon as you pick up a pen, however, you become aware of the screeching of countless gulls. At that hour it seems as though wanton female gulls are offering themselves in exchange for a crust of bread.

Around half past ten the first girls arrive, then the first men. One or two windows appear to be occupied already, but these early birds only receive regular customers at such hours. Only once did a scrawny girl, apparently wandering around by mistake at 9 A.M. in Bloedstraat—Blood Street—inform me in her heavy German accent: "I take it all off."

I've often noticed that the first men who arrive around mid-morning (many of them sporting mustaches) hang around the whole day. Most of these men—and how strange this is!—expend all their energy on a walk lasting from half past ten in the morning till late in the afternoon, without, it would seem, even once taking a break or going inside. I've been told there are even men who stroll past the windows, gaping, for fifteen solid hours, "spending the whole day doing nothing but window-shopping," as the girls say. You hear nothing but that curious, rhythmic, shuffling sound coming from inside, as though you were in Paris, listening to the sound of the subway rumbling past underground.

Most men apparently find their hungry journey past all those windows satisfying enough. They obviously don't need to go inside. At most they stop once in a while to ask the price. I've often overheard their whispered conversations. "How much?"

"Fifty guilders, sweetheart."

Then they'll walk to the next window and ask again— "How much?"—and be given the same answer. Sometimes such men ask the same question twenty times, only to receive the same answer twenty times. For some mysterious reason, however, some of the girls do it for half price, though there is nothing to distinguish these hookers—attractive or otherwise—from their more expensive colleagues. And the cut-rate price of only twenty-five guilders is apparently not even offered as bait to get a sybarite to set foot inside, only to hear, "Come on, hon, give me another twenty-five and I'll take off my top," because from the information that is often volunteered to me, I gather that such girls do in fact screw for half price. They also appear never to do it naked, but whether or not they take off their bra certainly doesn't justify a difference in price of twenty-five guilders. Why doesn't the Consumer's Guide take up this issue?

And so, simply because so many men limit themselves to window-shopping, their desire increases to the boiling point. The men saunter and stroll and once every hour and a half they seek relief in the urinal next to the Oude Kerk.

A real customer generally doesn't stroll. He appears with nervous, hasty steps from Warmoesstraat or Lange Niezel. He wears a hat, or a baseball cap pulled down at an angle over his eyes. Not infrequently he wears sunglasses to shield his eyes from the blazing sun. Quick as lightning he hurries past the windows. He makes a choice, stumbles in his haste on the stairs leading to a red-lit basement room, and falls bang into the arms of an elderly lady in underwear. Of course there are also men who arrive at a calm, measured pace and go inside in an open and honest manner, and these are also the ones who accost you on the street or suddenly fall into step beside you and tell you about their experiences.

Once I was accosted by an older man who asked me for a light. When I told him I didn't have one, he said, "Probably just as well, I shouldn't smoke so much, that way I'll have more money to spend on all this."

He made a sweeping movement with his arm and remarked, "I always come here nervous as hell. But, well, you have to. The night before, you feel like you've got your head stuck in the kitchen fan. You have that feeling, you know, that it's high time. And then you go, just like you go to the dentist. The crazy thing is that you're always a bit disappointed if you get one who's nice to you. Then again, you get pissed off if you go in and the bitch says to you, "Hello, darling, make it a hundred and I'll give you a blow job first." You get some experience, though, and pretty soon you recognize the real hustlers. Look, one rule is that the more they're wearing, the less chance there is they'll take all of it off. Or else you have to pay extra for every little thing that comes off. So never go in if they're completely dressed, take one who's wearing nothing but a bikini. Another rule is to choose one wearing high boots. She won't take those off, you can bet on that, at the most she'll stuff your money into them. But that doesn't matter; even if she keeps the boots on, she'll take the rest off, and if they're wearing boots, they usually don't hustle you. I don't know why, but they don't. Oh, and the chubbier they are, the nicer they are, but that's true in real life, too; it won't surprise you to hear that. Well, goodbye then, see you later, alligator . . . oh, wait, there's one more thing. If there's one with curlers in her hair and a hair net, you should go for it. You might think to yourself, I've got those curlers at home, standing in the kitchen, but you're wrong. Take the one with the curlers, man, then you've hit the jackpot."

Never, though, have I seen a girl in curlers sitting in the window. At the most they're using a curling iron and if you ask me they only do that in order to get in the mood. After taking up their position in the window, girls don't want a visitor right away. That's why they sit there putting on their makeup first. My authority was probably crazy about curlers precisely because you never see them in the red-light district. Many men, I've noticed, seem to walk around here searching for the ideal woman, whose picture they carry around in their minds.

In the café that burned down and has since been rebuilt, a drunk once told me, "I always say to myself, Pete, old boy, if one of them's smoking a pipe or a fat cigar, you rush right in."

"And was there one?" I asked.

"No," he said, "never."

"Maybe you tell yourself that," I said, "because you know you'll never see one smoking a pipe or a cigar. That way you're always safe around here."

"Are you crazy?" he said. "Get out of here."

Still, I think that man, just like many who share his fate, only yearns for a pipe or cigar smoker because it practically guarantees he'll never have to go in. When I first lived here, I also used to tell myself that I'd only go in if they met certain requirements. "If one of them's playing a record of a Vaughan Williams symphony, I'll go in," I told myself. Well, how likely is that? Later on, I often thought, "If there's a beautiful one sitting in the window, dressed to kill wearing a blue suit and an elegant blue hat with a veil, then I'll go in."

But what actually goes on behind those curtains that are always closed in such a hasty, slapdash way as soon as a customer enters? Once in a while a girl lounging in a doorway volunteers the information that she doesn't "do French." This leads me to assume that all those other girls do in fact "do" that language in the dark, something I gleaned from another remark I overheard in the burned-down café: "It's such a god-damn letdown when they start by taking out their false teeth."

Even the expression I found so intriguing at first—"with soapsuds"—probably only means that the man has asked for a blow job without a condom (costing at least twice the usual rate), which means his prick is first given a thorough washing in a derivative of Sunlight.

Once, when I was walking down Gordijnenstraat, a door flew open and a little man leaped out and disappeared like greased lightning around the corner of Monnikenstraat. A girl came running outside, crying out in despair, "He wanted me to shit on his face, can you believe it, he wanted me to shit on his face. I can't just shit on command, can I?"

I really feel sorry for such men. Imagine being cursed with a perversion like that. Even in the red-light district it seems there's no one who can help you.

Once I nearly succumbed. Early in 1982 I was walking, somewhat dejected, from the television studio to my house. I had just been confronted, during my appearance on Sonja Barend's talk show, with an extremely aggressive feminist. After the confrontation I had stayed and talked to her supporters for a long time. I had also had a bit too much to drink. I was walking down Warmoesstraat toward home, still all worked up about it, when I turned off at Sint Annenstraat, and cut across Dollebegijnensteeg (whose name, referring to medieval lay sisters with a reputation for loose living, could hardly be more appropriate). Halfway down the lane a young girl called to me from her red-lit room, "Come in and have a cup of coffee."

I suspected a trap as I took in the pretty young woman with her huge head of curls and white corset that made her body look conical. But I was dying for a cup of coffee.

"Do you really have some coffee?" I asked.

"Yes," she said, "I just saw you on that TV program."

She pointed to a fluorescent blue box with a long feeler sticking out of it.

"I'd really like to talk to you for a while," she said. "No one else will be coming along tonight, it's so quiet this evening. And I just made some coffee. Come on in for a while."

I inhaled the aroma of fresh coffee, braced myself, and crossed the threshold. As soon as I was inside she closed the curtains. Force of habit? Or did she have ulterior motives? She pointed to a narrow bed with a towel spread out on it.

"Take a seat," she said.

"Okay," I said, "but . . ."

"How on earth could you let yourself be taken for a ride like that?" she said.

"Well," I said, "even before the show started I could tell that woman had taken uppers or something."

"How could you tell?"

"From the pupils of her eyes. They were dilated and didn't react at all to the studio lights. So I thought to myself, no pupil reflex, she must have taken something strong like an amphetamine."

"What do you care?"

"Well, for one thing, you know that people who take stuff like that can get really aggressive and start acting completely anti-social. This was obvious, because she couldn't listen at all."

"You should have stuck up for yourself."

"No, I thought it would be better not to. I told myself to stay calm and not get angry. Otherwise, when I get worked up, I start spouting nonsense."

"You should have gotten angry. I was downright ashamed

to be a woman when I heard her going on like that. It was terrible!"

She poured some coffee and sat down next to me on the bed, saying, "I wrote a term paper about you."

"You did?" I asked, incredulous.

"Yeah, in college. I'm a college graduate, bet you didn't think that, huh?"

"No, certainly not."

"Shortly after graduation I came to work here. I could hardly wait. Once in a while I worked here secretly before I finished studying, but, you know, you're always afraid one of your professors will come along . . ."

"But with your degree, couldn't you find some other kind of work . . ."

"Are you kidding? Do you think there's any other job where you can earn as much as here? Or one that's this much fun? I love my job. Men have one-track minds, you know, there's nothing they'd rather do than . . . don't look at me like that, you know yourself you're just the same. And once they come into the room, and you get them really turned on, you can do anything you want with them. There's nothing more fun than squeezing as much money as you can out of a guy. A feminist like that should come here and have a look. Here it's the men who are exploited, not the women."

"No, they're exploiting you."

"Come off it, I'm only renting out my pussy."

"God, to think that a college graduate ended up here."

"Well, it's not as though I was forced into it. My father's rich. He owns a factory in Haarlem. My boyfriend was completely against the idea, but I wanted to get rich quick—really, really rich—and you'd better believe I'm going to do it."

"What about your boyfriend?"

"Oh, we broke up, I don't have a steady boyfriend at the moment, guess I'll find another one some day . . ."

"One who . . . oh, never mind."

"What do you mean?"

"Well, how should I know, I always thought that all the girls here had 'boyfriends' they handed all their money over to."

She burst out laughing.

"God, you're two thousand years behind the times. There's probably not one girl here who does that, no way. Most of us have a fifty-fifty arrangement."

"What's that?"

"Well, it means giving half your earnings to the person who owns the room you work in."

"That's not a bad deal," I said.

She poured me another cup of coffee, and said, "I wish I'd been there on Sonja's program, I would have smashed that woman's face in. If she were working here, her curtains would stay open the whole night. Even if *she* paid *them*, instead of the other way around, she wouldn't have any customers. That's why women like that have to brag about themselves all the time. They're not one bit attractive. They can't get anywhere with men. But I can get them to do anything for me, I can make them beg for it."

Apparently I looked skeptical, as she then said, "You don't believe me, do you? Don't you think I'm attractive?"

"I think you're very pretty," I said.

She put her arm around me, and said endearingly, "What

did you get for appearing on Sonja's program? How much did they pay you?"

"Nothing," I said.

"You mean you let them walk all over you for nothing?"

"Yeah, why not?"

"You really didn't get paid a thing?"

"No."

"What a pity. When you came walking along, I thought that Sonja had probably paid you two or three hundred guilders. But you do have *some* money on you, don't you?"

"I'm afraid not."

"You can't be serious! What about all those books you've written? You must be rolling in it. You must have a couple of hundred guilders on you! Give it to me and you can stay a whole hour. We'll have a fantastic time, I'll do anything you want. Business is slow tonight anyway."

"I don't think I have more than ten guilders on me."

"Poor bum, and all the time I was thinking how much you must have earned on that program . . . well, if only I'd known. And you don't even have any plastic . . . ?"

"Plastic? I thought those things were called rubbers."

"Not those, dummy, I mean plastic to pay with, a credit card or a check or something. Come on, you know what I mean. Write me a check and I'll pour you another cup of coffee and then I'll give you a blow job and . . ."

"I don't have any checks or credit cards with me," I said.

"But you live just around the corner. You can go home and get one. Go on," she said, giving me a nudge in the back.

"Okay," I heard myself say, with surprise. I got up and she opened the door.

"Don't forget to come back," she said.

"I won't," I said.

"Liar," she laughed.

"I promise I'll come back," I said, hurt.

"That's the way," she said as she pulled back the curtains, "I'll wait for you. I won't let anyone else in, not even Prince Claus himself."

I stepped outside. Two men were walking down the lane. One of them was saying, "Yeah, those writers nowadays . . ."

On Oudezijds Voorburgwal a cold wind hit me in the face. I couldn't believe what had happened. What had I done? Instead of going home, I walked along the water to Grimburgwal, and came back by the other side of the canal. By the time I got to Oudekerksplein I was filled with remorse. I'd promised her I'd come back—immediately— and back I'd have to go. At home I stuffed my checkbook in my pocket and quickly walked back to Dollebegijnensteeg, arriving at her window to find the curtains closed. A strange, almost sublime feeling of relief came over me, and I virtually danced back to my house, where I lay awake, content, for the rest of the night.

Translated by Diane Webb

Rambling around Centraal Station

Geert Mak

IT WASN'T UNTIL DAWN slowly brought color into the sky above the river IJ, that the world behind Centraal Station came to a halt. Most of the girls were still standing there; once in a while they copped a cigarette from us. Whenever a police van passed we ducked out of sight, but it was winding down, you could feel it.

"Scumbags, come over here!" called Hilga from The Hague after the Opels, the Volvos, and the BMWs that kept on cruising by. "It's going well, very well," Astrid whispered on her way back from her seventh client. "You know, Tommy and I are moving in together. We're getting a room. Together. At Het Hekeltje."

Hilga, in the meantime, with her short, stubby body, her boxer's face, her sweater that barely covered her crotch and her bare legs that were ravaged by wind and by life, had started walking right down the middle of the street. She hadn't had a single client all night. "Come on, boys, hey. Or do I have to take off my panties too?"

On the benches along the IJ, Jan and Marten lay sleeping—some rags, a few pieces of cardboard, a piece of an arm or a leg protruding here and there. Over by the water lay a few we didn't know, flanked by their bottles of fruit wine. On the loading dock, right along the central platform of Centraal Station, Tommy sat drinking a beer with some Belgian guy. And Rick and I were taking Gina home. Gina, who can roar like a hurricane, who whores half the canal area single-handedly, steals and cadges, and who afterward walks arm-in-arm with you, skipping and chattering like a schoolgirl.

It had been one of those remarkable long nights in May that Rick and I wandered around the city together: Rick, because he had to, because he didn't have a roof over his head, hadn't had one for years; me, as a kind of luxury tagalong.

First we hung around for a while in the warmth of Centraal Station. Like every night, starting around midnight, all six telephone booths in front of the main entrance were in constant use. Anyone who had scored some heroin went in there to smoke or shoot up. We found Gina and Jan there—"Leave us alone for a minute, Rickie, don't you see we're busy"—but there was also a seemingly well-dressed girl who, as soon as she was inside the booth, did some sleight of hand with a cigarette lighter, discreetly pushed her skirt up a little, and with a practiced gesture eased the needle into her thigh.

In the nearly empty station we watched the last hurried travelers while the sweeping machines were already well into their rounds. There were maybe fifteen homeless Moroccan boys leaning against the columns and the walls, some of them still in early puberty. Among them sauntered an older gentleman. It was a wordless process, on those stone floor tiles of that big hall, a kind of chess game of looks and small gestures. The man suddenly made for a boy, and in less than a second there were two fewer chess pieces in the hall. They are cheap, those boys, I later learned. A twenty-fiver for a whole night of action, maybe two or three hours of sleep, breakfast, and then back onto the street. Twenty-five guilders. But at least you have a roof over your head for a while. "Only the very young can make more. Sometimes up to fifty guilders, if they've just run away from home."

*   *   *

Now it's well into the day. "Come on, let's move," says Rick, and we walk on. We cadge a cigarette, cop a brew, and we keep on walking. When you first arrive in this city, you're homeless, and when you're homeless, you can only do your thing in a few places. Everywhere else, you have to pay. So it's walk, sit, hang out, wait for nothing, and then back to walking, because you have to do something.

Almost everyone on the street has a story: drink, drugs, a divorce, a run-in with the law. Some come from psychiatric institutions, others are here illegally and simply don't exist for the rest of society. If you don't watch out, once you're on the street, you quickly end up in a cycle of poverty, in an increasingly grubby and tramp-like state. It's almost impossible to escape from this, since no employer and no landlord will have anything to do with you anymore.

This Legion of Dishonor in the city consists of a few thousand men and a hundred or so women, but the academicians have been quarreling for years over the exact numbers. Ever since anyone can remember there have been just a handful of women; it's pretty much all men. "Every woman has a you-know-what, an eternal moneymaker, and things have to go pretty badly for that not to bail her out," the guys say with envy.

Rick is an unremarkable, dark man of medium height with a lean face and a dash of Indonesian blood in his veins. I know him from a former life. Things haven't gone well for him, and even on the street he has remained a misfit. Once upon a time he was involved in social work. He went through two divorces, was turned out of his home, hit bottom, and on top of that, he had fallen ill. He told me all this on a rainy afternoon while we were waiting for the open air Albert Cuyp market to close for the day. He described the situation you drift into when you end up on the street as an inevitable downward spiral. "Your first inclination is to move to a big city," he said. "It offers the most opportunities to get food and it also has the most of the kinds of places where you're left in peace."

After that, however, or so I gather from Rick's stories, a rather Kafkaesque situation arises. The first few months—and for some that can last one or two years—you can't get welfare benefits because as a homeless person you don't have a permanent residence. On the other hand, you can't get a room or other permanent residence because you have no money. "So now you're completely stuck. And then you deteriorate quickly."

The welfare problem can sometimes be solved with so-called "postal addresses," or official residences. This could be some kind of charitable institution, but it could also be a commercial boarding house, a café, or a gambling hall. Usually they charge exorbitant rates, sometimes up to hundreds of guilders a month, and as for charities, it comes with all sorts of conditions, which most of the guys don't care for.

Even without money though, it's possible to keep yourself reasonably afloat in this city. While we were talking, five o'clock came around. The merchants were taking down their stalls with a lot of noise and clatter, and before our eyes, we observed the emergence of an alternative shopping style. Bruised oranges, overripe mangoes, peppers, cucumbers with small tears: it all got stuffed as quickly as lightning into plastic bags by casual passersby. In the end there were at least fifty people rummaging through the garbage dumps behind the stalls. This happened quickly and efficiently: obviously everyone had done it before, and everyone knew that you had to do it quickly, or the merchants would start to yell and curse.

A few well-dressed mothers with children were busy behind a stall that sold oranges; an elderly man found a brownish bunch of bananas on the street; and a bit farther on down, a skinny, half-naked boy wearing shorts was eating a piece of raw fish over a garbage bin. On one street corner a small-scale, covert exchange market had started up. "I've got two cauliflowers to spare. Have you got any fruit?"

Every day the garbage pickers visit the market in waves, so I'm told. It starts as early as four-thirty with a few young women and the odd elderly person, those who are not so readily turned away. Then, at five o'clock, the usual group of completely or partially homeless fan out over the market. Finally there is another group that doesn't make its appearance until five-thirty. They are so filthy and unkempt that they would be sent packing immediately if the merchants were still at work. That's why they end up trudging behind the garbage trucks at the very end of the market day, hobbling along in their rags, sometimes on bare feet.

For the hungry the city offers more places where something can be had. At the fritters stand, which moves around from place to place in the city center, they always put a large garbage bag filled with old fritters outside around closing time; soon afterward, you can see shadows move in on it. Then there are the Augustine sisters at Warmoesstraat, who distribute packaged bread. Very popular is Mother Teresa, at Egelantiersstraat. Every day at a quarter to four and at four-thirty there is a long queue of men and the odd woman. Inside, in a large bare eating hall with long tables, a meal is served daily to about two hundred of Holland's poor by a couple of Indian nuns. They do this modestly, without even the slightest hint of condescension, and I suspect that this is the main reason why they are so popular, even among the guys who want nothing to do with the ministrations of other charitable institutions. Almost all of us mumble along with the prayer at the beginning of the meal, eyes tightly shut, in ragged coats, old jackets, some wrapped in blankets: "Holy Mary, Mother of God, pray for us sinners, now and in the hour of our death."

At Mother Teresa the quality of the food depends on what the nuns manage to pry away from various stores and restaurants in Amsterdam that day. There are days when everybody suddenly gets a hamburger, or meat and salad, others when there is only bread and some thin soup. The times that Rick and I ate there it was usually something in between: a kind of thick soup made of root vegetables with pieces of sausage.

Once after the meal we got a huge piece of raisin bread with raisins and nuts. "Expensive raisin bread, good raisin bread," muttered our neighbor across the table, and soon the conversation turned to the quality of the other eating establishments at the bottom of society. At Hare Krishna you can also get a free meal daily, but they always have the same thing, my tablemates complained: "Rice with chopped cauliflower, carrots, and curry sauce." The Salvation Army has frozen meals, but you almost always have to pay for them. Everyone agreed that by far the best meal is served once a month at a place called De Wallen by a minister. "You can get a good meal there, three courses, and you even get a bag of oranges and a roll of peppermints as you leave," our tablemate across from us said. "But you do have to first sit through a church service, at which his daughter plays the guitar."

Translation by Tineke Thio

Staring Out the Rear Window

Hermine Landvreugd

GOOD THING we could barely hear the bands. I really don't like the blues. We'd set up the stands on the muddy edge of the festival grounds, close to the portable toilets and the parking lot full of dozens of gleaming motor-cycles.

"What are you charging?" a thirty-something in denim asked. He tucked a lock of ropy hair behind one ear.

"Depends," I said. I'm going to act just as sassy as I look, I thought. Get tough, you weak-kneed bitch, otherwise the telemarketers will never stop bugging you once your trial subscription runs out.

The guy pulled a can off a six-pack and offered me one. I said no thanks. He shrugged and sat down on the table, shoving a pile of T-shirts to one side.

"Put your money on the table, or get your ass in gear," I said.

Sissy Boy, who was unpacking a box of baseball caps behind me, snickered.

"Smarty-pants, huh?" the thirty-something nodded approvingly. "I like that. Why don't you go over to the field with me; your buddies can watch the shop. Little Feat starts playing in an hour, and we can get right up in front."

I put on my Walkman and whistled loudly to Tricky. I hoped he couldn't see me shaking. Sissy Boy was doubled over laughing. I walked past him through the opening in the tarp to the other stand, where Inse and that other boy, the one whose name I always forget, were selling sunglasses and those fanny packs that Hans makes. The fanny packs were selling like wildfire.

Thirty-something had circled around and was standing in front of me again. Goggling at me, legs wide apart, tugging at his beer. I started arranging the goods. He said something, but of course I couldn't hear him. Suddenly he grabbed me by the arm and pulled me toward him hard, so the edge of the table jabbed me in the stomach. His flushed face was right up close to mine, I could see the little red pimples on his nostrils. He hissed something through his teeth, grinned, and licked me across the lips: a long, wet, slobbery one. I pulled away from him, but at that moment, he gave me a shove and I fell over backward. With one wave of his arm he swept all the merchandise off the table and walked away, laughing.

Inse and the other boy helped me up. SB stuck his black pompadour through the split in the canvas. He lifted the phones off my head. "I was pretty amazed, but I didn't want to say anything," he said. "I couldn't help laughing, but you've got to be careful, you never know with these blues retards." He brushed the sand off my butt. I rubbed my arm where the nutcase had squeezed till it hurt.

"For the same money, that geek could have jumped on his bike and crashed through the stands, with us in them."

"Right," Inse laughed, "a typical SB fantasy. Whenever something's happening, he makes sure he's in the back row, but he always knows how to beef up a story. You read too many comic books, SB."

SB and I picked up all the fanny packs and sunglasses from the ground and wiped them off with a dishcloth. Inse and the other boy went to get hot dogs and a few cans of beer.

"You know," SB said, "there's nothing wrong with being so assertive, right, especially not for you. I mean, sometimes you have to. But you can also turn the tables on them."

"What do you mean?" I picked up a fanny pack that had fallen right next to a bag of french fries covered with mayonnaise.

"You can take advantage of the fact that the guy wants something off you. And you can get paid for it." He said it casually, so I couldn't tell whether he was joking. But the tense way he waited for me to say something meant he was serious. That told me enough already. I knew SB would have done it for money. Just to get his goat, I didn't say a thing.

A gust of wind blew in wisps of a whiny guitar solo. I stretched. "Listen to that garbage. What do they see in it?"

"Right," SB said, and I could hear his impatience. He put on a pair of sunglasses he'd just cleaned. "But what do you think?" he started in casually. "About people who rent themselves out for you-know-what?"

"Everyone should use their body parts as they see fit," I said.

SB laughed, but he still looked tense.

I couldn't figure out why he cared what I thought. I looked straight at him. "So what's it to you, anyway?"

He started stammering and blushing. "Well, I just, uh,

you know, we're, I mean we've been working together for a year now, we're more or less friends, right?"

Once we were back behind the stand he said, "I do it sometimes, at festivals too. I just wondered whether any of you had noticed."

"Not me," I said, and SB seemed to take that as a compliment. He beamed. "I've got to admit, I'm pretty slick about it."

"Shall I take this one or this one?" A boy in pink leather hot pants was striking a pose with one leg crossed in front of the other, his hand on his hip. "Maybe none of them will look good on me," he sighed, "what do you guys think?" He shook back his long, wavy hair and kept his eyes on SB. "I mean, maybe they'll laugh at me. I'm real sensitive about that, you know?"

SB stared straight back at him. "Hard to know, really, but why don't you try on a few behind the gents'? Wait, I'll help you." He grabbed a pile of T-shirts from a box. I think they were all the same, Pearl Jam logo, medium.

They made their way past the motorcycles, heading for the toilets. Inse and what's-his-name didn't even notice. Inse was trying to put on three pairs of sunglasses at once, and what's-his-name yelled something at him that I couldn't hear, then buckled over with laughter.

"Singin' in the Rain," SB was humming. We were in the back of the van, sitting between all the soggy cardboard boxes. The cloudburst had come before we'd finished taking down the stands and putting the stuff away. The rain rattled on the roof and ran down across the rear window in little winding trickles. It was dark, and the only thing I saw were the headlights of the cars behind us. The hairy brown mat I was sitting on pricked my butt; the floor of the van shimmied pleasantly.

Driving home is the nicest part of the job, at least that's what I think. I wrapped my arms around my knees; I could imagine being anywhere in the world.

"Hold up your lighter here." SB was trying to roll a joint on top of one of the boxes, crumbling the hash onto the paper. When he was done, he realized that the rolling paper was stuck to the box. "Shit!" He kicked the box hard, and it fell over.

One of the guys up in front knocked on the back wall of the cab. "What's up?"

SB stared straight ahead and didn't say anything, his hands folded between his legs. When we pulled off the freeway, he almost fell off the spare tire.

I couldn't help laughing.

"What's up?" he snarled. I didn't understand why he was so grumpy all of a sudden, and I didn't feel like getting into an argument.

"Did you make any money off of that guy?"

SB pulled a banknote from his pocket and smoothed out the wrinkles. "Blow job with a rubber."

"Who blew who?"

A tired sigh. "Me him, of course."

I've taught myself to stare straight out the rear window when I'm in the van, so I can't see the signs saying which town is how far away. Nagorno-Karabach suddenly popped into my mind. I had no idea where that was, but I'd probably heard about it on the news. It sounds mysterious, Oriental. Right away I imagined the smell of incense and that all those headlights out there were the Rolls Royces of oil sheiks, chasing us because they all wanted me in their harem, of course. "SB, Nagorno-Karabach, imagine we're there and . . ."

"No thanks," he cut in on me, "I don't know if you ever read the papers, but there's a war going on there. Sorry," he went on right away, "but I don't have a place to stay anymore. I don't think my boyfriend's going to let me in. I ripped up his napkin with the Anni-Frid and Agnetha autographs. My parents won't have me either. And then in this rain."

"So stay at my place."

He hugged me right then and there and gave me a big fat kiss on the cheek. "That's so sweet of you. And it doesn't even matter to me whether you know about the war in Nagorno-Karabach. But if you ask me, I'd rather be in Ducktown. In Ducktown, tramps have a right to free hamburgers and cokes, did you know that?" He looked at me, glowing.

We came into the east side of town under the railroad trestles. Hans, our boss, the one who makes the T-shirts, lives at the city's edge. In the very last block of houses on the street, behind the purple curtains on the fourth floor, his was the only light still on. The rain had almost stopped when we started unloading the van. Hans must have heard us pull up, because he stuck his head out the window. I could see his double chin, which I always think is pretty gross.

"Hey, sweetie pies," he shouted and his voice sounded flat and hollow in the empty street. "Look out, here it comes!" He threw down the key to the basement door; it clattered on the stoop. "Don't trip, the light's broken!"

"And you're too cheap and lazy to get it fixed, right?" Inse mumbled as he picked up the key.

"Did you say something, Inse?"

I pulled my coat sleeves down over my hands and picked up a pile of boxes from the bottom so they wouldn't fall apart. We took it all down to the basement without a word.

"Just put it down anywhere," Inse gestured broadly. "You can't see a thing anyway, so it's not like it has to be neat."

The basement stank of damp walls, the way it always did, and I bumped into the open door of the washing machine.

When we went back out, Inse slammed the basement door behind him and locked it. At that very moment, Hans raised his squeaky window again. The curtains were hanging in front of his face like a veil. "Finished? Good work, kids. Inse, will you bring the wallets up here?"

Inse stuck out his arm like a hat rack and we all hung our money belts on it.

"Did you fill up the van? Change the oil?" Hans yelled.

SB said, "The first oil rigs were built in 1857, in Pennsylvania. Before that time, people found oil only by accident, and used it for medicinal purposes. As a patent medicine. Good for indigestion, balding, eczema, and promoting miscarriages. Until someone discovered its utility as a fuel, and the oil rush was on."

I looked at him in amazement, and he said with a grin: "*Lucky Luke,* episode 18. 'In the Shadow of the Derricks.'"

"Did you say something, SB?" Hans shouted, and when SB didn't answer back he said: "SB, come up with Inse. I want to talk to you for a minute." The window went down, the curtain was pulled closed from the inside, and after a moment the door clicked open.

What's-his-name said see you, and walked away.

Inse waited in the doorway for SB to come over, but SB said, "Catch you later, Inse, I'll go up some other time." He grabbed me by the arm and dragged me around the corner.

"Wants to talk to me. Wants me to sit on his dick is more like it." He raised his hand and flagged down a cab.

At nine o'clock SB shook me awake, and from that moment on he refused to leave me alone. He wanted to pick up his things at his ex-lover's.

"Hurry up a little," he kept saying impatiently, "hurry up, please, let's get it over and done with." He already had his coat on. Wet, freshly washed tufts of hair were sticking out from under his cap, and he smelled of soap. We sat at the kitchen table, I blew on my tea to cool it down, and he whistled and drummed with a fork on the butter dish.

I ate a biscuit while he stood beside my chair, holding a toothbrush with a ribbon of toothpaste on it.

When I went to get a towel from the closet, he looked so disappointed and sighed so deeply that I didn't take a shower after all; I just sprayed my armpits with Ocean Fresh deodorant. That really stings on unwashed skin.

On the way to the tram stop, SB tripped along in front of me, spinning and twirling a roll of garbage bags like a majorette. At the stop he kept on cutting patterns in the air with the roll of bags and balancing on the curb and humming "ta-ra-ra-boom-dee-ay." I looked the other way, put on my Walkman. What was I going to do when summer was over and the festivals stopped? I was hungry.

After six or seven stops, we climbed out and took the

crosswalk in the direction of the Concertgebouw. Our shapes were reflected shakily in the windows of the glassed-in foyer.

The hall was hidden behind two entrance doors and completely done in sea-green tiles. We snuck down it.

"Natural reaction, isn't it," SB smirked when he saw how carefully I was putting my feet down, "in an environment where you don't belong."

We stepped up to the door on the left, which was flanked by two shiny copper pots full of cattails and purple- and green-painted plumes.

"He couldn't find everything in exactly the same color as the tiles; man, was he pissed," SB grinned as he opened the top lock. Then his eye fell on an envelope stuck between the door and the doorpost. "SB" was written on it. He tore it open and read out loud: "SB. You realize that you can't live here anymore. Please leave the key in the mailbox. Take only what belongs to you. In other words, don't steal anything. No offense."

"Don't steal anything." Insulted, SB pushed the door open. "So there you have it, my former lover sees me as a common thief in the making." As soon as I stepped across the threshold my feet sank into the piggy-pink shag carpeting. SB sat down in front of the Bang & Olufsen sound system in the living room and started looking for his CDs and tapes. He hesitated before putting an ABBA CD in his garbage bag. "What do you think: is it stealing when you take back something you gave someone? But if I take this CD, that actually means I have to leave all the CDs he ever gave me. And there are about twenty-seven of those." Deep in thought, he turned the ABBA CD over and over in his hand. "Or does fairness count when it comes to matters of the heart? I'll just take everything. I mean, you know the old proverb: 'All's fair in love and war.' And proverbs always contain a kernel of truth, right?" He looked at me expectantly. I told him I was the wrong person to ask, I didn't know anything about proverbs.

"Well, at least that's clear," SB gave an exaggerated sigh. "Ethical dilemmas are wasted on you."

My stomach growled. I decided to look for something to eat in the kitchen. With SB jumping around like that all morning, I'd eaten only one biscuit instead of my usual three.

On the marble counter was a toaster that still felt lukewarm and next to it, four orange peels all tucked together. I always think it's rude when people go around opening all the cupboard doors in a strange house. Fortunately, at that moment I saw a plain wood breadbox. Next to it were at least ten packs of Perla Mild coffee from the Albert Heijn supermarket, and on the windowsill I saw a big silver fruit bowl decorated with half-naked angels and filled with kiwis, mangoes, and bananas. There was also a piece of exotic fruit I didn't recognize, an elliptical thing with bumpy, reddish-orange skin. The door of one of the cupboards above the counter was open a crack anyway, so I reached in and took out some cherry jam. On the shelf in the middle, SB's ex had stored another thirty or so packs of Perla Mild. I sat down at the kitchen table on one of the calfskin chairs and enjoyed my food. Just when I was thinking about opening the fridge anyway for some milk and luncheon meats, SB called to me.

"Come here, in the bedroom! Come see how happy we were! Oh, no, don't tell me!" he added, sounding upset. "Oh, no!"

I put the bumpy-skinned fruit back on the dish so you couldn't see right away that I'd taken a piece of it. Bland and sourish, not very nice.

"So, what was it you wanted to show me?" I plopped down on the big bed with its purple velvet spread and glistening stars. Wonderful soft bed. I was a little bit drowsy from getting up so early, and with the breakfast I'd just had, I could have conked out there for an hour or so. I stretched out and made myself comfortable.

"I should have known. Of course he wouldn't let any grass grow under his feet. The slut makes these posters with all his little-ass boyfriends. God, it's so sick." He kicked an antique-looking chest of drawers, the candelabra in the shape of a Greek hero holding two bowls fell over, and the angora cat that had just stuck its head through the door jumped away in fright. "I'll deal with you later, shit cat," SB snarled at the animal.

"Shall I tear it up, what do you think?" SB pointed at the pink-edged poster stuck to the door. The middle of the poster was a big heart-shaped photo of two naked men embracing, in soft focus. Below the heart, in decorative gold letters, were the words "Eternal Love."

"It looks like a real David Hamilton," I said, examining the poster up close. "Is it a real Hamilton? Think of what that's worth, man. Wow, pretty romantic." I ran my hand over the poster. "Those letters are even embossed!"

"Will you please just shut your fucking face!" SB screamed, red with annoyance. "I don't know whether it's

sunk in yet, but there used to be one of these posters here
with the two of us! I'm barely out the door and he's got one
with his new little whore of a turd-burglar!" He wanted to
rip the poster off the door. I was barely able to stop him.

"Don't do that, man, it's a Hamilton, it's worth thou-
sands."

SB sank down on the bed. He turned up his nose. "It's
not a David Hamilton. It's from the Albert Heijn supermarket." He pointed to the lower left-hand corner and, yes
indeed, there it was, real small, the AH logo.

"You buy ten packs of coffee and you get to make one of
those posters. You have to send in the picture yourself. And
pay fifteen guilders." He searched around under the pillows,
found a box of tiger-striped condoms and threw it out the
window. "That'll be dry-humping for them tonight." It
didn't seem to make him feel any better. He drummed his
fists against his thighs. Screamed: "Do you know how long
that takes, before you get one of those posters back? Three
to five weeks, which means that sneaky, backbiting little
gay-pride pixie . . ." He buried his face in his hands and
began to breathe deeply.

SB went to pee. When he slammed the door, first I heard
the cat give a horrible shriek, then paws scurrying down the
hall, then the clatter of the cat door.

He's lying on my bed, staring at the map of the world.

It seems like he doesn't notice me standing in the
doorway.

"I'm leaving," he says without looking at me. "I'm going
to Scotland. Next week. This time of year the big estates are
always looking for people to help with the hunt. Tossing

dead deer on the back of a horse. First they spend three
months shooting the stags for their antlers, after that the
does, to keep things in balance." SB kicks off his sneakers.
"Can't you picture it?" he asks, acting cheerful. "Me, the former whore, XTC junkie, and queer, on the hunting estate
of some rich old sod? Yes sir, of course, your wish is my
command," he bows deeply, "my ass is yours, sir, whenever
you please." He bursts out in peals of laughter and falls back
on the bed. The laughter turns to sobbing. I'm looking right
at his gym socks, the toes and heels of which are dark-
brown with dirt. Who's going to wash them for him when
he goes to Scotland? I lie down next to him, caress his shaking back. "I love you, Sissy Boy," but it's as though the twilight swallows up the words.

Sissy Boy nestles up against me like a child. With a finger
I trace the lines of his dry lips, and we kiss until our faces
are completely wet from each other's tears and spittle. You
don't get it from spit. Besides, I don't know whether SB
even has it.

I decide to play it safe anyway. Once SB is asleep, I roll
him carefully to one side. I wash my face thoroughly with
disinfectant soap, Unicura. Then I apply a Dr. Van der
Hoog deep-cleansing mask and lie down on the coach, listening to Candlelight. I try not to sing along with the
words, because then the mask would crack.

Translated by Sam Garrett

The Light at the End of the Tunnel

Gerrit Komrij

I

JACOB, IT BECAME CLEAR to his fellow pupils and his
teachers at school, had a darned poetic nature. Some class-
mates were even concerned by the way he would always
have his nose in a book and his head in the clouds. And he
would fill up every scrap of paper, no matter how tatty, with
his scribbling. But there were teachers who took pity on
him. One of those teachers advised his parents to take him
out of the Hogere Burger School, where he was studying
business and economics, and send him to the Gymnasium,
where he would study classics and the humanities. Jacob
quite liked this idea, for with a Gymnasium diploma he
would be able to study at the university in the city, later on.
Besides, only lower-class people studied at the Hogere
Burger School anyway. The students from better families
were at the Gymnasium.

His parents agreed to this. They were proud of the fact
that he had caught the teachers' attention. But wouldn't it
be too much of a burden for him to catch up with all those
studies? Why no! Jacob assured his parents that he would
set about it with a vengeance. After all, wasn't that the big

city luring him from afar? Though his time at school would indeed last two years longer now, it remained the only possibility to reach the city whose name alone filled him with a shudder of awe: Amsterdam; Nineveh, Amsterdam; Babylon, Amsterdam.

There he was, during the summer holidays, cramming in three years of Latin and two of Greek. In two months he would have to be reading Xenophon and he didn't even know the Greek alphabet yet. He studied eighteen hours a day. Conjugations and reams of words. Exercises and cases. A new world of chariots and centurions, of obols and Punic Wars, stealthily marched in.

Jacob had to memorize his Greek primer up to the page that showed a photograph of a stone archway: the Lion's Gate. Beyond it lay freedom. But he wasn't anywhere near it yet. One hundred pages still separated him from it, then ninety-five, then ninety. His approach was slow. The gate became his obsession. At night he would dream that he passed through it, roaring, mane waving, and that he dropped down dead right on the other side.

Indeed, after eight weeks he was close to exhaustion. It had been like sewing with a red-hot darning needle. But he had become a Gymnasium student. In his head, the simplest *mensa mensae mensam* still whirled in brotherly fashion alongside the most complicated of aorists or dactylic tripodies.

That first year in the Gymnasium, he was already translating Greek and Latin authors. He didn't understand much of it at first, but he could not bear to leave a sentence undone or write the kind of verbiage most pupils used when translating: "repairing the while they saw" and "on learning meanwhile that." He Dutchified his Ovid with an adept hand; he would fashion a splendid phrase of his own invention even though at times it would turn into quite a different story from the one told in the original.

"You're like Berlage's Stock Exchange," his teacher grumbled, handing back the test papers. "The building's splendid but the foundations are rotten."

How he would beam! If they compared you to a building in a city, even if it was a palace built on quicksand, a rose with rubber roots, then you were almost *in* that city.

He would have to stay on at school for two extra years if he was to end up as a student in Amsterdam. He would gladly suffer this for that. Then, the year he took his finals, the stipulation that a Gymnasium diploma was required to attend university in his chosen field was lifted: the deferment had been in vain. That was the way of the world. You jump fences others are taking down; you surmount barriers that are ready to crumble. Those coming after you find only scrap iron and dust, not barriers. Things would always be better for you if you took things easy. But then how would you have learned to jump?

Why was it that Jacob wanted to go to Amsterdam so badly that he was willing to plough his way through a mound of Pindar and Plato? He could have gone to a sleepy provincial town like Utrecht or Groningen. Not on his life! Every fiber of his body pointed, like the needle of a compass, toward Amsterdam. But why, oh why?

Because of sin, first of all. Sin he didn't even know and that was as hidden as it was highly promising. Something

in that city lured him, though he didn't know what. He was
driven to go there, but it was the blind instinct of a mind-
less cow, if you looked at it closely.

These were the years of dark desires, of unexplained signs
and feelings. Jacob did not know the journey's destination,
yet each time he knew the road he must take. "Following
his nose." He didn't know what he sought, but he was sure
he would find it.

His parents had observed with concern how he recoiled
from such beautiful places, beneficial to both peace and
study, as Utrecht and Groningen, as well as the immovable
direction of his magnetic fibers, and they took measures.
Together with a school friend, the son of a preacher, he
would live at the YMCA that provided "young men" with
room and board. They would be able to keep an eye on him
there, his parents reasoned, and he wouldn't slip into irregular eating habits either.

His room was above Centraal Hotel and looked out over
the Leidsebosje Municipal Gardens. The city lay at his feet,
humming and teeming with all the temptations he didn't
know, but which doubtlessly would come.

For the time being, virtue still ruled within the walls of
the YMCA. Jacob lived there among students and other
boys. (The concept of young people having a job had not
been invented yet.) They sat at long tables and ate rice with
peas, and gruel for dessert. There were corridors with many
doors opening onto them. The residents of each corridor
elected a representative from among themselves. This representative's task was to see to it that everyone obeyed the
rules. Karel was the representative of his corridor. At half
past ten in the evening, Karel, a compulsive busybody of a

boy, with pimples and a whopper of an Adam's apple, would give a tremendous bang on his door and without waiting for a reply, open it and stick his head in. He had to make sure there were no visitors in the rooms anymore. It wasn't allowed after half past ten. Rules of the house. Karel never missed a single evening and was never a minute late. He performed his tasks with devotion. Half past ten and there was the bang, followed by the head. Later, Karel would end up writing a poetry collection called *Droning Gnomes*.

Jacob wasn't that bothered by the banging. At last, he thought, he was free. He could now go out and walk around as much as he wished, return to his room when he felt like it, feed himself at the oddest hours, in short, the true wind of studenthood blew through his lungs. "Youth spreads its wings." From then on he could behave as debauchedly as he wished. And that, indeed, is how he *wished* to behave.

For the time being, he had only a literary notion of debauchery. Sin consisted of daydreaming about seventeen-year-old boys with raven hair and moist, brown eyes who rowed him down the Amsterdam canals in golden gondolas and, surrounded by bunches of grapes and acanthus leaves, fanned him with fern fronds. Sin consisted of taking a walk, in his mind's eye, through a poppy field with a big, handsome moor, his black, oil-anointed chest gleaming in the morning sun and thunderous, devout spirituals resounding from his mouth. That kind of sentimental tosh. These, as always, were still cardboard cut-out fantasies.

Jacob, however, knew one thing for certain: there was a secret circle of people in Amsterdam who practiced this sin and debauch with full abandon, and it was into this circle he would now penetrate. The only thing was to make the first contact, and then he would be sucked up further and further into the circle, as of its own accord. He felt like a mouse running up and down along a wall searching for the hole behind which the world of cheese would be revealed: mild and strong cheese, Gouda and aged, lush Edam and nifty cubes, cheese stretching as far as the horizon: a world of mousely luxury.

Jacob had once read—he no longer knew where—that all the inhabitants of the secret circle wore suede shoes. The first time he turned into Leidsestraat—like an explorer clearing a path through a jungle without knowing where it would lead—he peered at the ground, continuously. Not like an explorer, really more like a ragman. And surprisingly, he saw many suede shoes. Wearers of suede shoes were actually in the majority, by far. It was as though he saw nothing but suede shoes. Clearly this had to be a red herring.

A few days later, on Geldersekade, close to the Waag building, he discovered a café called Friendship. There it was written on the window in large ornate letters. His heart was beating in his throat. That had to be it: the mouse hole! Five, six hours he stood across the street, waiting for a sign of life. At last, the door to the café opened and two drunken sailors fell out, each accompanied by a woman made entirely of hair spray. For a second time he had allowed himself to be led down the garden path.

He would have to start all over again. Diligently he went on searching for the little tunnel that would lead him into the other world, the world of cheese and sin. He was so taken up with this search that he did not even realize how miserable he was: such a touching, desperate mouse.

It seemed as though the sinful world he sought did not wish to reveal itself to him, as if the circle remained closed and would not surrender its secret. Did such a world, such a circle, actually exist? He knew of its existence only from magazines and books, and maybe everything had changed since their publication. Perhaps that world had indeed existed for a short while, but had dissolved, been subsumed to the ordinary world, become utterly secret. After all, you couldn't see a green chameleon against a background of nettles, now could you? That being the case, you could search until you were blue in the face—or you might have found it already without knowing it.

He had been living in the city for two months and hadn't made any progress at all. He had often followed groups of boys or an old man who looked eccentric, but they would always disappear into gray stairwells, trams, or cars. What did such people actually look like? Even of this he had no idea.

Ye he calls upon, O goddess of the pavements, O spirit of the Amsterdam gables. Many a sole did he wear out upon thee, many a time didst thou see his shadow roam bashfully past thy faded countenance. Down here there is not a cobble of thine he has not trodden, no window sill across which his shadow has not been cast. All that time, O muse, thou hast led him to the middle of nowhere and thou, O spirit, laughing with scorn, hast reflected back the flickerings that stirred thee when he stepped between thee and the silent lampposts. Ye both doth he curse, for answer gave ye none!

And all the time that Jacob trudged on out there until deep into the night, another spirit floated alongside him, a spirit who had seen it all before and who had reached into the farthest corners of all those domains, to Jacob so unknown. This spirit was as silent as the tall shadows, as speechless as the cobbles and the lampposts—it was his good genie who could not reach him and therefore wept bitterly. If only he had not been so possessed with searching for the gateway into another world and had not been so taken up by his presumed paradises, had not roamed about with a look so full of unhappiness and question marks, then perhaps he might have felt his genie drop a tear on his neck from time to time, like a big droplet of pain. This spirit, who floated above the waters and the worlds, who saved the human being he had been assigned from the dangers of the deep morass, and shepherded him with an invisible hand past the vacuum of the ravine so that he might safely see out over the peaceful valleys—this spirit knew with a spirit's clarity and certainty that he wasn't on his way to dens of sinful pleasure but to dives of vulgar drinking; that there he would not encounter ephebes but rather greasy queens; that he would trade his innocence for fleeting obscenities, his hope for dark jealousy, his beating heart for dubious teasing jabs; and that he would squander his boy-sweetness for a drink.

Jacob had deserted his good genie, cruelly cast him off, so full was he of that impossible urge to find comrades, *doppelgänger*—and the genie wept.

11

The café was deep and narrow, an oven darkly glowing. Everything seemed red because of the red of the padded walls, the velvet bar-stool covers, and the wide open shirts of the serving boys who moved jerkily back and forth behind the bar—like dolls in a weather box or a clock. They bent over a customer—for a moment they gave the impression of having been talking like that for hours—in a relaxed and confidential pose, but a moment later, a few yards away, in an identical pose, they would be giving an entirely different customer the idea of having an intimate conversation. And all the while they pretended not to be aware of everybody looking incessantly at what was being emphasized by that pose encapsulated in red silk. Everything was so red that even on a summer's evening someone in this café might believe himself to be in a warm stove. Assuming he was inclined to spend an entire summer's evening in a warm stove, that is. Lots of people didn't. Frequently they didn't have the figure for it.

But Jacob had crept through the fire door and was now sitting at the bar, a fiery ember with an overheated imagination. From the jukebox rang out Maria No Más, The Young Ones and Summer Holiday, Adamo and Dinah Washington. In a niche, high up behind the bar, stood a gigantic bunch of roses, flouting all earthly proportions. Beneath it, a yard-long run, like a narrow tube, had been made of chicken wire, and scores of chicks were wandering around inside it. It was Easter. The swarming chicks were intended to be a festive sight. Compliments of the management.

The stove was filling up more and more. Now, too, the cinders of the night sidled in. Little was said but there was much winking and pinching. Each time two embers touched there was a hiss. There was an exorbitant amount of looking, exorbitantly shameless. And the doorman stood at the fire door and occasionally allowed someone to slip in hurriedly and turn red instantly.

He sat on a stool, held on to the bar, and looked very dour. He feigned indifference. His expression was gruff because he dared not let it be friendly. He didn't really know how to burn.

It was completely full now. Everything seemed to take place more slowly at this time of night. Hands slid down legs. The boys behind the bar now seemed to be standing still while spending time on a customer, glances remained fixed on someone longer and more piercingly, embraces lasted forever, and even the chicks began to move more slowly as though they were ashamed to be so orange-yellow in red surroundings.

There was a small sitting area in the corner of the café. A lamppost had been put there that, like the bunch of roses in the niche, clashed with all sense of proportion. It had to have been an incorrigible optimist who had lugged this post inside. It spread a fearsome coziness. A red coziness, never fear.

And all this red light shone on the faces of the boys and men who shrieked, cackled, drew wet trails of slime with their tongues down another's cheeks, ordered lots of Dutch gin over ice, checked repeatedly whether their dyed hair was still looking just so, spread clouds of cologne, and stood draped against the wall in amazing positions, zigzagging night flowers, snakes with broken vertebrae, badly made jigsaw puzzles.

So this was it. It was getting hotter and hotter. Arms hung round his neck. He felt a cheek rubbing against his. Never had Jacob felt so happy and unhappy all at once. There was no possibility of escape now: he would have to let himself go. There was a lump in his throat that wouldn't go away. There was a rushing in his ears. But he had to enjoy it, like it or not.

Suddenly, right in front of his eyes, the flames flared up high. Away—he had to get away. He was being gobbled up by the red. But he did not go. He didn't walk out onto the street. He continued to sit there staring ahead, beatific and perfectly brainless. Quiet. It was comfy here. Here is where he would have to burn up, for the rest of his life. He was doomed to this fire. The strange hands on his stomach were burning. Beads of perspiration pearled on the chests of the boys behind the bar. The red was now the red passing before his eyes. The embers danced in the flames. The chicks had become roasted chicks ages ago.

Everything went very quickly now and soon Jacob knew every bar, every meeting point, and all the codes, identifying marks, and peculiarities of the people who came there. He was living in a city within the city; in a matter of months he was following, almost sleepwalking, along the paths laid out between the fixed points of the shadow city, and he would only move along that spider's web of paths. It was a fixed circuit, a ritual.

In the past, standing in front of his bookcase, he would sometimes fantasize about how it would be if there were a lighting system that emitted messages from that bookcase: for instance, were he to think about the subject *Middle Ages* or *large size shoes*, all books featuring the Middle Ages or shoes of a large size would light up so he would be able to see them instantly in the bookcase. He would also know at a glance which books had been published in the year 1906 or which volumes had been in the possession of boys with melancholy hands and a bent for poetry. Somewhere in the bookcase a light would also flare up from the book that, after his death, would most fiercely provoke the greed of his as yet unknown heirs. Thus the light combinations would dart about like the billboards on which the same light bulbs present different messages each time: first a bottle, then *Ooooo!* and subsequently *Drink Coca Cola*. Like at the fun fair. This time only one lamp in his bookcase would light up; the next time a light would shine forth from many books: and where it would come from exactly would always be a surprise. He had command over all information at any moment, factual and abstract. Such a system would make life more pleasant.

That's how it ought to have been in the case of the spider's web of the city within this city, he thought, now that he noticed how extensive it actually was. If an electrician had plunged everything into darkness and lights had come on only at all the points of more or less fleeting encounters within the web and if he had then flown over the city, he would have been able to see it in a flash: the blinding, widespread network forming a world unto itself. It would make ordinary people, in their ignorance, sit up and take notice. Only by means of such a play of lights could you make them face facts, when all was said and done. That's how the secret would be brought to light, the existence of which they had not suspected, that's how the extraordinary would be emphasized, and lines drawn. He felt himself to be quite the light-bulb magnate.

For the time being, his nonsensical thoughts were accompanied by equally nonsensical behavior. Every evening, before diving into the web, Jacob would powder his face, draw black eyebrow arches to a point just above his nose, and paint his lips dark red using powder compacts, crayons, and lipsticks tailored to his budget.

From the five-and-dime.

The scent of lavender and green soap battled for supremacy on Jacob's body. His nails, fraternally, displayed both mourning and silver glitter. Besides being a light-bulb magnate, he was, in his own opinion, a true master of the mascara brush, but in reality he was a bungling splotcher. The doll he had become didn't resemble him at all anymore.

It was fortunate that no bulbs lit up at each item of his new disguise that had something amiss, something hopelessly wrong. He would have looked like a Christmas tree.

There was no secret, merely the suggestion of the secret.

For a long time he lived in the mistaken belief that the world he had discovered was the only true one. All that happened in that world was done right. With the eagerness with which a mother cuddles her child even if it has four goat's legs and a piggy tail, he surrendered himself to it. He behaved as though he had cobbled that world together himself; with great zest he made all the specialties of its puppets his own. He was there, always and everywhere. If someone was silent, he would be more noiseless still; if someone cried out, he would cry louder. That he did all of this out of slavish gratitude at being allowed to belong was not apparent to him yet. For the time being, in his perfect camouflage and to his own constituency, he appeared most content.

From now on the dull outside world could only count on his contempt. That the outside world thought this quite terrible, he was sure. He neglected his former friends and his studies; the moral rules of that miserable real world that wasn't even real met with his haughty rejection. Those rules too suffered greatly because of this: one knew that right away.

In his world everything was better: everyone resembled one another and everyone acted the same; he only needed to look around him to feel in the company of like-minded ones; all were as one in their contempt for the "normal" world, as it was scornfully called. Lordy-lor, how much better they were. Normal? It was the very worst that could befall you. They were, happily, all different together.

Jacob's camouflage had only just barely begun to wear off when he messed things up at the YMCA. At first he would occasionally, furtively, take some trade home, via the entrance to the Centraal Hotel. He would pull a face as if he were staying there—a stupid face, that is—and step into the elevator with his acquisition, plunging headlong into a petting session right then and there, for this was the custom in his world. If, in the evening, he had visitors in his room and it was almost half past ten—the time at which the droning gnome began his *hongi* expedition, his crusade against moral subversion—Jacob's visitors would hide under the bed and he, the book inevitably held upside down on his lap, would pretend to be studying. He had only a small single bed but, without the gnome detecting anything at all, four sizable characters could fit underneath it, necessity being the mother of pliability. But soon—his camouflage was marching on toward perfection—he began to think this hide-and-seek preposterous and, painted and powdered, lugging along a raving queen with a heavy Amsterdam accent, he strutted around the recreation areas of the Young Men's Christian Association.

The chief gnome of the Association summoned him and told him he was to vacate his room by next day. This because he transported himself illicitly in an upward direction by means of the elevator belonging to the adjacent hotel. The doorman had lodged a complaint against him. He, however, understood the true reason all too well. Clear as anything. He had to get out because so much withering scorn for gnomishness shone from his eyes. It was nothing but this wigmy-pigmy's jealousy, just because he had to crawl into bed beside an old bag with curlers every night. That young Christian man of forty simply had no part in the exciting circuit of those who were so very different. That's what it was.

Thank God he did belong. Even if he was homeless now, that feeling was shelter enough for him.

With probably the last bit of sense he had left, he set out in search of new digs.

Translated by Richard Huijing

Flesh and Blood

Bas Heijne

HIS MOTHER OPENED THE DOOR. She was wearing a
red, tight-fitting dress he had never seen before. Her face
looked different as well; short hair made her look younger.
Hello, son, she said with pride in her voice. Come in. You've
lost weight. It suits you. She squeezed his hand as he
stepped over the threshold. He did recognize her smile.
She looked like an ambassador's wife.

He kissed her carefully and followed her in through a
wide passageway with a low ceiling. This is still only the
hall, she said. Feel this. She took his hand and rubbed it
along the wall. Just like velvet, she said. Isn't it soft? She
gazed with awe at the dark blue material.

There were doors down both sides of the hall. They
looked like empty picture frames. The door handles were
made of brass. Soon, said his mother, who had noticed his
glances. First the living room.

His father was in the living room. He was sitting in a
leather armchair with a tall glass in one hand. When they
came in, he looked up with surprise, as if he hadn't realized
that a visitor had arrived. He was wearing a white shirt
with the top button undone and a red tie. He too had his
hair cut short and looked years younger. Son, he said. I had

no idea it was so late. He put his glass down on the table and planted a dry kiss on his son's cheek.

Well, he asked. What do you think? Be honest.

The living room was like the hallway: low and wide. Around the glass table stood chairs and a soft white leather couch. The walls were white too and hung with pictures in big chrome frames; he recognized a lithograph in the Cobra style. Through the glass doors at the end of the room, he could see planter boxes full of red and purple flowers.

It's big, was all he could come up with. A lot bigger than you'd think. Enormous.

Yes, his mother said, incredible. To tell you the truth, we're still getting used to it ourselves. You don't expect this much space in an apartment.

What do you want to see first, asked his father, the other rooms or the view? It's up to you.

While he was still thinking how to answer, a piercing alarm went off somewhere inside the apartment. He saw his mother jump. The new dryer, she said apologetically. That means it's done, at least I think it does.

She disappeared quickly into the hall.

His father walked over to the balcony door. He rapped on the glass. It gave off a dull, vibrating sound.

See, double glazing, all of them, he said. You hardly hear a thing, not even from the street directly below. And it's not just the noise; it saves on heating too. The only problem is, they're tinted. To be honest, that's something we don't really like. I don't know why he did it. Because of the sun, probably. Around two o'clock it shines right in. I guess he wasn't a sun lover.

He slid the door open silently. They stepped out onto the balcony. The light was blinding. His father stuck out his hand and pointed.

There, to the left, you can see the Amstel River, he said. And that's the Amsterdam Woods. Look.

He tried to follow his father's hand but was so startled by the height that he instinctively grabbed the railing. Below him, he saw car roofs in the parking lot.

While his father pointed out Utrecht, he imagined himself plummeting over the balustrade. He would fall and fall, splattering on the shining metal below. He pictured his head bursting open; everything he had ever thought would be gone, gone forever.

For a moment he saw his own body lying there beneath him. Mangled flesh and blood, red-saturated clothes. One shoe off.

He suppressed his dizziness and concentrated on a toy windmill between the flowers in one of the planter boxes. His father talked to him. The plastic blades moved back and forth in the wind but didn't turn. He wondered how the windmill had gotten there.

His mother was back in the room behind them. Well, she asked, can you see the Amstel?

He turned toward her and nodded. Yes, he said, his dizziness gone. It's fantastic.

His father put a hand on his shoulder, and they went back inside. That was our garden, he said. Now the rest of the house.

They walked down the hall, and his father opened one of the doors. This is my study, he said with a grand gesture. Sometimes I sit here alone for hours. See those chairs? Five

thousand guilders apiece. The desk was already here as well.
It only needed waxing.

Look at that, said his mother, pointing at the ceiling.
Look how beautifully that's been done, she said. Cornices
everywhere. And the wallpaper. It's so beautiful.

The man had *taste,* said his father. Everything top quality. Only the most beautiful was good enough.

Yes, said his mother, so sad. When you think about it.

The door opposite the study led into the kitchen. He
blinked: white marble everywhere, on the floor, the walls,
the countertops. His mother opened a cupboard and triumphantly pulled out a shelf mounted on rollers on which
she had arranged cans and boxes and pots. The refrigerator
and freezer were hidden behind a wood cupboard door.

Look, said his father. He pulled a banana off a bunch in
a bowl on the counter and pushed it into a hole in the
gleaming steel sink.

There was a loud metallic grinding sound.

Gone, said his father. Nothing left. Handy, huh? I didn't
even know such things existed.

They looked at the other rooms one by one: their bedroom, the guest room, a spare room, the toilet. He watched
his parents walking around their new home like tourists
in a museum. It's magnificent, he said over and over.
Magnificent.

He felt the tingling coming on in his left leg.

And now I want to see the bathroom, he said quickly.

Silently his father and mother led the way down the hall.
The bathroom was behind the last door on the right, next
to the living room and opposite the guest room. Here, too,

there was white marble everywhere, and mirrors: on the wall above the two sinks and on the ceiling. A two-person bathtub was sunk into a platform at the other end of the room. To step into it, he saw, you had to first climb four marble steps. There were mirrors mounted above the bathtub, and against the back wall stood a big copper vase, without flowers.

He looked up and saw his own eyes, small and scared.

What luxury, he said, running his fingers through his hair. Decadence. A Roman bathhouse.

We want to get rid of those mirrors, his father said. It's a terrible sight when you're sitting in the tub. Every time you lean back, you get the shock of your life. You're all red and shriveled. I don't understand how anyone could come up with an idea like that.

It takes a faggot to think up something like that, he said.

His parents were silent, embarrassed.

It's true, he said sharply, at the same time ashamed of his aggressive tone. Then he shrugged. A normal person just doesn't put mirrors up over his *bathtub*.

You haven't got mirrors above your bath either, said his mother. She sounded hurt. The cheerfulness with which she had opened the front door was gone.

Maybe I can take these off your hands, he said. Suddenly he grinned widely, as if it had been a joke all along.

They ate at a table he recognized: it was from the house he had grown up in. My name must be somewhere under here, he said. He went down on his knees and felt around for the familiar, scratched-in letters. He thought he found them, but it was too dark to see anything.

His mother started to tell him how to cook Belgian endive in the microwave. A few minutes on high with just the water left from washing, and more vitamins were preserved than when you cooked it in a pan. He already had one of those things, why didn't he use it? Even his father could manage it. He cooked quite often these days, not like in the old days when he was still working and didn't even know how to boil an egg. Well, the occasional egg, but that was it.

Do you cook much for yourself at home? asked his mother, who had noticed that he wasn't listening.

He put the hot endive in his mouth and swallowed it, feeling it burn its way down. Not often, he said, lately, hardly at all.

You have to be a bit careful about what you eat, said his father, holding his fork up in the air.

You can get fresh vegetables in restaurants too, he answered slowly.

He had heard it all so many times. In the past, when he was still a student, he always had to defend TV dinners. Now it was restaurants, about which they had even less cause for complaint. Nothing has changed, he thought.

His leg was still tingling. Under the table he squeezed his calf with one hand. He didn't feel a thing.

Your flowers look nice, he heard his mother say. She pointed behind him. He turned and saw big red flowers in a vase on a marble pillar, carefully lit with a small spotlight. The flowers were arranged as if they were part of a stage set.

Staring at the thick red petals, he felt the blood rush to his face.

Flowers?

Had his mother's words been ironic? He didn't remember giving her any flowers.

Panic raced through his mind. Red flowers? When? Where? At the door?

Of course, at the door. He always brought flowers. Now too. Of course he had. He tried to summon up an image of himself pressing them into her hands on the way in.

He tried to hear the crinkling tissue paper.

Son?

His father's voice.

He turned back. His father and mother were looking at him with such fear and concern that it sobered him.

I was thinking of something completely different, he said, making his voice as detached as possible. I thought . . . I had to think about our old house.

Your mother and I drove by there last week, said his father. They've completely plowed up the garden. There's a little pond there now with a stone bridge. Seriously. They've put a plastic heron next to it.

This was familiar territory.

A *plastic* heron, he said, glad to have found something in common.

At least it's better than a garden gnome, commented his mother. You still see them all over our town.

Hardly, he said in the tone they were used to hearing from him. It's hardly better than a garden gnome.

His parents laughed carefully.

I'm so glad to be rid of that garden, sighed his father.

Somewhere beyond the hallway a bell went off. His mother stood up.

Dessert's ready, she said.

His mother showed him his bedroom. She made him feel the curtain material, and she demonstrated the bed, an

Auping. It's wonderful for reading, she said, pulling a cord that raised the head of the bed.

He stood there for a moment after she left the room. The tingling in his leg had crept up to his groin. He sat on the bed and took off his shoes. Carefully he massaged his extended left leg. In the light of the big overhead lamp the flesh above his sock looked unhealthily pale.

Dead, he thought. Dead meat.

He pinched hard and flinched from the pain.

He picked up the towel his mother had laid on a chair for him. In the hall he heard soft voices in his parents' bedroom. Just like in the old house, he thought. His bedroom had been next to theirs and whenever he woke at night with a bad dream and walked across the landing to go to the bathroom, he would hear them talking in subdued, reassuring voices.

He stood still for a moment in the dark hall to listen, then got scared he might hear them talking about him.

In the bathroom, the marble shone dully. The previous owner had installed small light fixtures with dim bulbs all over so the room looked as if it were full of a thin golden mist.

Here, he thought. This is where it happened. He quickly undressed and started washing in front of the tall mirrors. He tried not to look at himself. He splashed water onto his face, as fast and as much as possible. He grabbed a washcloth and hurriedly lathered his armpits. Then he carefully wiped around his groin, scared to feel anything.

Was that his glands? Were they swollen?

He dried himself off, then pulled his boxer shorts back on and combed his hair. He folded the towel and picked up the rest of his clothes. Then he stood there looking at the empty bath.

For a moment he imagined it, like in a movie, a thriller. The full tub, the steam from the water. The body: submerged, pale and swollen. And blood of course, blood everywhere. On the marble steps, in long red finger stripes on the tiles on the wall, great red clouds in the water.

Clots on broken glass.

He switched off the light and walked back through the hall to his room, carrying his clothes in a bundle. He jumped when he opened the door. It was pitch black inside. But he clearly remembered leaving the overhead light on. Had his father or mother just been in here? He couldn't see a thing. At home his curtains were thin; the material his mother had praised so highly had all the transparency of a wall.

He put down his clothes and shuffled over to the bed until he bashed his shin against it. In the darkness he felt as if the pain were someone else's, as if his whole leg had nothing to do with him. He sat on the edge of the bed and waited while the dull ache spread along his bones, momentarily displacing the tingling.

I am alone, he realized suddenly. There's no one to help me.

Strangely enough, the thought was a relief. He lay down on the bed without groping for the bedside lamp and decided to go straight to sleep. He slid in under the blankets and lay on his back, determined not to think about anything. But his mind was too clear. He was shaken awake by an image of the body in the bath.

After a few minutes his left hand slid down to the elastic

of his boxer shorts. Involuntarily he slid his fingers under it and began to massage the soft flesh at the top of his leg.

Did he feel anything?

He kneaded the other side, unsure whether there was any difference. He felt it again, and again. His fingers began to pluck at the wiry hair. Could he feel something? Did it hurt?

He felt something.

I'm going to die, he thought. I'm going to die. I know it.

He imagined the apartment's previous owner, the expensive man with the expensive things.

The man unlocks the front door and comes in laughing, followed by two dark youths. He's wearing an elegant coat with a velvety sheen (feel this, he heard his mother saying); the dark youths are dressed in battered leather jackets. They whistle when he turns on the hall lights.

The man takes a bottle of champagne out of the fridge in the kitchen; from one of the cupboards above the sink, he takes three glasses. The youths whistle anew. So many expensive things; it makes them quiet but also angry. The man leads them to the living room, pops the cork triumphantly, and fills their glasses to brimming. He watches them greedily gulp it down. He feels tender and fatherly at the same time.

This is the life, he says. The words sound strangely out of place in his own home.

The expensive man and the dark youths drink and drink, and the young men get quieter and quieter while their anger grows. Slowly their fury fills the room. When the bottle of champagne is empty, the man sends one of them to the kitchen to fetch a new bottle. In the meantime he goes and sits next to the other one and puts his arm around him. The youth comes back in with a new bottle and lets himself drop onto the sofa next to the man. They kiss and stroke each other and the man smells the cheap leather of their jackets. When the man unbuttons his pants, one of the youths suggests getting into the bath.

A fabulous idea, exclaims the man. He lets the youths undress him and walks naked to the bathroom with the bottle and his glass.

Eyes closed, he wondered when it went wrong. At which second or fraction of a second did the young men's anger win out over the expensive things around them?

He stayed there, lying on his back in the dark room, and thought of the naked expensive man in his bathtub on the other side of the hall. He now had both hands underneath the elastic of his underpants.

It happens at the moment the man takes off his Rolex and lays it on the edge of the bath. Without the watch's gold, he suddenly looks defenseless, a victim. The youths have undressed as well and ascended the marble steps. They are sitting naked with their legs in the water. They look at the watch on the side of the tub and at the pink man in the steaming water and they see how weak he is, how helpless without his watch. They see that the man and his expensive things do not belong together. He's sitting there like a poor creature, begging for what they have too much of.

He's sitting there as if he's nothing at all.

They look at his body in the hot water and see themselves naked in the mirrors on the ceiling. Their anger swells until it's bigger than they are. When the man holds up his empty glass as a request, one of the youths looks at the other and smashes the neck off the bottle.

He started. How long had he been asleep? His hands were still under the elastic of his underpants. He looked for the clock next to his bed, then realized that he was in his parents' new apartment. At the same moment he remembered his dream, that was true, a dream that wasn't his or his parents', but this apartment's. For a second he felt like the man in the bathtub on the other side of the hall, defenseless, with just as little idea of what was in store for him. Then he groped for the bedside lamp.

The light made him blink.

He got up and walked out of the room, looking for the toilet. In their bedroom, his parents were silent.

Translated by David Colmer

Business

Lizzy Sara May

A SATURDAY AFTERNOON in November. As an exception my mother had gone shopping alone with Josje, who suddenly needed a new pair of pants. My father was home, sitting at the table and reading a paper.

On Saturdays the children were supposed to be at home because my father insisted on having us around on his days off. This was an attitude that I, as a child, didn't understand at all. Sundays weren't as bad; then we usually went for a walk or went visiting, or someone came to visit us. But those Saturdays! Then God's Eye rested upon us and demanded that we be quiet, obedient, and sweet. This meant that we couldn't really play, that at every shout my father's eyebrows would be raised, that we would have to make up for lost time—not spent tormenting each other—on other days.

Now that Mother and Josje were gone, the room was straightened up, and my father was reading, a heavy boredom pressed down on me. If only my mother were home. Every moment that she wasn't sitting at the piano, she was willing to read to me or tell me a story. My father knew only one: the fable of Brownie the Fox and Reynard the Bear—as a silly joke he switched the names—plus a story called

"Tante Mijntje" by Herman Hijermans, which he read with
a lot of dramatic feeling, pinching his nose to accentuate the
polyp in Aunt Mijntje's nose.

Because my father's storytelling only took place on
important holidays, I didn't dare ask him to do it on that
dreary November day. So I sat down in front of the window
and stared outside.

First a peddler of oranges walked by, and then a short fat
man who glanced up at me as he passed. Right after that
the bell rang. A moment later Frieda announced that there
was a gentleman for the gentleman.

My father got up and proceeded to the front door. He
came back into the room with the short fat man whom I
had just seen.

"So, you're here for business," said my father as he sat
down. "Please take a seat."

But the short fat man came toward me and pinched my
cheek. "What a fine girl."

It hurt.

"My daughter," my father said with obvious pride.

"Mazel tov," said the short fat one. "How old is she?"

"She's six," said my father. "She's already in first grade and
can even read and write."

That was a slight exaggeration, for I hadn't yet mastered
the whole alphabet. But I didn't contradict my father
because I too thought I could read and write.

The short fat man said: "Dear God, what a blessed child!"
and sat down.

"And what is the reason for your visit, Mr. Cohen?" asked
my father.

"That I'll tell you," Mr. Cohen said brightly. "Do you
know Bram Katan?"

"Bram Katan?" said my father. "You mean the one on Weesperstraat?"

"No, that's Sol, the pots and pans man who is married to a Mietje Meier. No, I mean Katan on Lepelstraat."

"Katan on Lepelstraat," my father reflected. "Isn't that the son of the old Katan on Waterlooplein?"

"That's him—you've got it!" Mr. Cohen exclaimed. "That old Katan is a second cousin of my wife."

"So who's your wife's family?" asked my father.

"My wife is an Augurkiesman," said Mr. Cohen.

"Not on Jodenbreestraat?" asked my father.

"On Jodenbreestraat . . . on Jodenbreestraat? Wait a moment, aren't those the Augurkiesmen who are in textile? Yes, sure. No, my wife is from Nieuwe Keizersgracht."

"Oh, now I know!" said my father. "Those are the Augurkiesmen who used to have a small business on Jonas Daniël Meijerplein. Is that your wife's family? Then I even worked with her at Van Dam's diamond polishing shop!"

"No, that's not my wife. My wife was a seamstress. Her sister Chellie was a diamond worker. My wife's name is Roosje. But what I wanted to say, Mr. Maai . . ."

"May," my father corrected.

"Do I care? May," said Mr. Cohen. "Aren't you related to the Maais on Damstraat?"

"Well, family and *mishpoche* are two different things," said my father, "that's one of my father's second cousins . . ."

I was still sitting at the window and was sick and tired of the conversation. I could just as well go and play outside since my father had no time for me anyway. I started to yawn, and, as if summoned by fate, my friend Ansje appeared at that moment in front of the window. She pressed her nose flat against the window in order to look inside, then straightened up again and shouted: "Hey, are you coming outside to play?"

Frightened, I signaled her to be quiet. Over my shoulder I looked at my father. But he had started talking about a certain Goudsmit and offered Mr. Cohen a cigarette, which the latter refused with a grimace: "I smoke only cigars."

As unobtrusively as possible I crept away from the window and tiptoed to the door. I could still hear my father say: "Then are you perhaps . . ." Hurriedly I pulled on my coat and ran to the front door. At the very moment I stepped outside, a fire engine drove by, bells ringing violently.

"Fire! Fire!" screamed Ansje. "Come with me to watch the fire!"

She grabbed my arm and together we ran to where the fire truck had disappeared. We were lucky, for the truck was standing in front of a house only one street away. A number of firemen had gathered in front of the door; they conferred and looked up. From the roof of the house a wisp of black smoke curled up. We wormed our way through the crowd until we were standing right in front. Ansje danced with excitement.

"Great, isn't it, nice and scary!"

I didn't think it was great, just scary. I myself had experienced a fire at home when the alcohol of my toy stove caught fire. Again, I could see my mother beside herself, running into the kitchen to get Frieda. Josje, just awake from his afternoon nap, stayed behind. I ran after my mother. Frieda filled the bucket with water, and the three of us ran back into the room. Josje, in the high chair next to the window, looked surprised at the flames that were extinguished with a splash from the bucket. My mother, her knees still shaking with fear, collapsed in a chair and started to cry.

"You know," Ansje said, her cheeks bright red, "I once saw a great fire, a giant blaze, and then lots of people, burned black, were carried down the ladders."

I shuddered.

"And when they were down, they fell completely apart, like burned paper."

I looked at her. Disbelieving. She might be two years older than me, but I felt that was no reason to fib.

"You're fibbing," I said.

"Am not," said Ansje, "just ask my mother!"

Of course it was all talk because I would never dare ask her mother. But I still wasn't sure.

"You're still fibbing," I insisted. "People never burn in houses. They are always pulled out by the firemen."

"Pff, you're such a baby! As if the firemen always come in time. Some children must have been playing with matches."

I winced and thought of the girl in the book *Struwwel-peter:* she played with matches, burst into flames, and only her shoes were left.

I looked up again. The black smoke had disappeared. The firemen were climbing into their truck.

"A chimney fire," said someone behind us. His voice sounded disappointed.

"You see," I said, relieved, to Ansje, "a chimney fire. No people were burned at all."

"I didn't say *now,*" Ansje defended herself. "Before, I said."

The fire engine left again, bells loudly ringing. We headed home.

Back in our street, my throat tightened. There would be the devil to pay because Mr. Cohen had of course left a long time ago, and my father would have discovered that I had disappeared.

"Shall we go to the Sports Park?" asked Ansje. It was very tempting to postpone my father's scolding look and sermon. But on the other hand there were Ansje's sinister stories. In addition, by staying away longer I would increase my father's wrath even more. I therefore said, "No," and reluctantly moved toward the front door. I had left the door ajar in order to be able to return as soundlessly as I had left. I took off my coat and softly opened the door to the room.

What I had expected—an angry face appearing over a newspaper slowly being put down—did not occur. The first thing I heard when I opened the door was my father's voice: "But that means that my father and mother were at your father and mother's wedding!"

"And isn't your father the cousin of my mother's second cousin? A Goldman. Dear God, Mr. Maai, to think that we're actually *mishpoche!*"

"Knock on wood," said my father. "Would you like some more tea?"

"Please," said Mr. Cohen, "all that shmoozing makes you thirsty. What a doll that child is! You don't hear her at all."

"Absolutely," said my father, and he turned to look at me. Meanwhile, I was again sitting in front of the window.

"Go and ask Frieda for another pot of tea, my sweet."

And to Mr. Cohen: "By the way, what did you actually come for?"

Translated by Jeannette K. Ringold

The Decline and Fall
of the Boslowits Family

Gerard Reve

MY FIRST CONTACT with the Boslowits family was at a children's Christmas party at some friends'. There were paper napkins on the table, with merry little red-and-green figures printed on them. In front of each plate burnt a candle in a socket carved from a half potato turned cut-edge down and covered neatly with dull green paper. The flowerpot holding the Christmas tree was covered the same way.

Near me, holding a slice of bread over the flame of his candle, sat Hans Boslowits. "I'm making toast," he said. There was also a boy with a violin; while he was playing I almost had to cry, and I thought for a moment of giving him a kiss. I was seven years old then.

Hans, who was two years older, began wiggling the branches of the Christmas tree with seeming nonchalance, until a branch above a candleflame began to sputter and emit a sharp scorching smell. People shouted, mothers came scurrying, and everyone near the tree was forced to sit down at the table or go to the other room, where a few children were playing dominoes on the floor.

The two Willink boys were there, too. They were the sons of a learned couple who let them go about with close-cropped heads because they were of the opinion that man's appearance is not the essential thing; this way it was easy to keep the boys' hair clean, and no valuable time had to be spent combing it. The cutting was done monthly by their mother with the family clippers—an important financial saving.

It was nice having the Willink boys around, because they would dare to do anything. Sometimes on Sundays they came with their parents to visit us. Then I would go out with them to wander around the neighborhood and follow their example by throwing stones, rotten potatoes, or pieces of horse-dung through every open window. A wonderful fever of friendship would liberate me from all my fears.

At the Christmas party they amused themselves by holding a burning candle at an angle over someone's hand or arm until the hot wax dripped on the victim's skin and he jumped up with a scream.

Hans Boslowits's mother saw it and said, "I don't think that's nice of you at all." But his father smiled: he admired the ingeniousness of it, and he didn't have to be afraid that anyone would try the joke on him, since he was an invalid, his whole lower body crippled by disease. After that evening I was to call them Aunt Jaanne and Uncle Hans.

I was very anxious to watch Uncle Hans leave, because I had seen him carried in by two other guests and the spectacle had fascinated me. But at half past eight, already, I had to go home with my parents.

Four days later, it was still Christmas vacation, I went with my mother on a visit to the Boslowits family. The street had a long, narrow stretch of grass down the middle, and we had to walk round it. "Well, big guy Simon," Uncle Hans said, "Hans is in his room. Go play with him."

When I entered the room Hans asked, "What do you want?"

"To play with you, that's what your father said," I answered, taken aback.

He had on a pair of knickerbockers and a green sweater, he was wearing glasses, and his black hair was plastered down and parted sharply. I looked around the room and caught sight of a small statue on the shelf above the convertible bed; on touching and smelling it, I found it to be a little dog made of soap.

"I made that," he said.

"Oh?" I asked. "At school?"

"By myself," he claimed, "at home, out of soap from the store." But I had already stopped believing him, because he had been confused for a moment by my question.

On his desk was an object that he kept looking at and picking up in a way designed to arouse my utmost curiosity. It was a metal box in the shape of a writing tablet, two fingers thick and a bit slanting, with a push button at the top. The cover was surrounded by a frame with a transparent celluloid window in it. You could write words on the plate. Not only with a pencil, but with a stylus that wouldn't write otherwise, or with a stick; the words appeared in purple beneath the little window. If you pushed the little button everything that had been written disappeared. The possibility that such a thing could exist had never entered my mind.

I myself was given the opportunity to write on it and make what had been written go away with a push on the button. Sometimes, though, the contraption refused to work, and the text remained wholly or partially visible.

"I'm going to throw it away," said Hans. "It's broken."

"It's a nice thing you can write on and it goes away when you push on it," I said to Aunt Jaanne, who came in just then. "Hans says he's going to throw it away."

"Now he's being bad again," Aunt Jaanne said. "He's going to throw it away because he doesn't want to give it away." All afternoon I kept hoping to possess the contraption, but I didn't dare make any reference to it.

In the living room, too, were interesting objects. For example there was an armchair that was six feet long, covered with leather and resting on one round metal foot. Because of its easy-to-damage construction I was only allowed to lower myself into it sideways; then I could use my right arm to turn a wheel underneath, whose position determined the angle of the seat.

On the mantelpiece stood two old delft tiles, one depicting a fisherman, the other a skater. Potted plants in little antique copper pails lined the windowsill—there was a small indoor palm tree, and any number of cactus plants, including a ball-shaped one covered with rope-like growths that Aunt Jaanne called "the plant with gray hair."

We sat down to lunch, and we had knives with yellow ivory handles. The blades bore an elegantly engraved trademark with the letters HBL. "What do these letters stand for?" I asked, but my mother, Aunt Jaanne, and Uncle Hans were so engrossed in conversation that only Hans heard the question.

"The H is for Hans," he said loudly, "and the B is for Boslowits."

"And the last letter?" I asked, waiting.

"But the L," he went on, "yes, the L!" He ticked on the

knifeblade with his fork. "What that's for is known only to my father, me, and a few other people." I didn't want to bear the responsibility of asking something that there were weighty reasons for keeping secret, so I held my tongue.

After the meal there was something new: a woman came with Hans's brother Otto. I had already been instructed about him by my mother: "The boy is a little backward, so if you dare tease him . . ." she had said.

"Here we are again!" the woman called out, and turned the boy loose like a dog given the liberty to jump up on his master for a moment. He stooped forward when he walked, and he was wearing extraordinarily high shoes with toes that pointed in toward each other. He had on knicker-bockers, like his brother, and he was perspiring so heavily that strands of his colorless hair were plastered to his fore-head. His face was strangely wrinkled, and his eyes didn't match.

"Well, are you here again, my little fellow?" his father said.

"Yeah," he called, "yeah, yeah father mother!" He kissed them both, and Hans. Then, standing still, he suddenly jumped into the air so hard that everything rumbled.

The violence frightened me, but he appeared to be harm-less, as my mother had already told me.

"Go shake hands with Aunt Jettie," he was ordered, and after the words had been repeated for him several times he succeeded in bringing out "Aunt Jettie" and "hello aunt," until they finally got him to say the combination, "Hello Aunt Jettie."

"And this is Simon," said Aunt Jaanne.

"Hello, Otto," I said, and shook his sopping-wet hand.

He jumped into the air again and got a piece of candy, a bonbon Aunt Jaanne stuffed into his mouth. Every time anyone asked him something—in the usual way, without expecting an answer—he would shout "Yeah yeah," "Yeah mother," driving the words out forcibly. Someone put a portable phonograph on the table, and the woman who had come with Otto wound it up.

"He stayed dry last night," she said.

"Oh, that's good, what a good boy, Otto; you stayed completely dry, didn't you?" his mother asked. "Isn't he a good boy, Annie?"

"Yes, he's been a good boy, haven't you, Otto?" the nurse answered.

"What do you say now?" his mother asked, "—Yes, Nurse Annie."

"Yes Nurse Annie." After an endless struggle he got it out, all in one breath.

He was busy sorting out phonograph records from a box. He held each one up close to his face with both hands, as though he were smelling it. His nose was red and damp, with a small yellow pimple at the end of it.

"He smells which ones they are," explained Uncle Hans, helping to sort from where he sat in his chair.

"This one," he said, and handed one to Otto.

The boy took the record, inspected it, sighed, and leaned on the table with his elbow for a moment; unluckily he happened to lean on a record, and with a quick little sound it snapped into thirds. I shouted something, but Uncle Hans took the pieces and looked at the label, then said, "A very old one, Otto."

"Old one!" Otto forced out, and put the record that his father had indicated on the turntable.

It was not like the other records: it was brown and thin and looked as if it was manufactured of cardboard or paper. Only one side was playable. Hans put a rubber piece on the turntable rod, because the record bulged upward a bit. When it started to play, a flat voice said, "The Loriton Record, to which you are now listening, is suitable for recordings of every sort. It is light in weight and flexible, and it is three times as durable as the ordinary record."

Then the speaker introduced a dance orchestra. When it had finished playing the voice said, "The Loriton Record can only be played on one side, but if you will check with your watch you will see that it plays twice as long on one side as an ordinary record. And, ladies and gentlemen, it's half price."

Otto was jumping up and down with impatience. His mother quickly chose another record, a small one with a pink label. Two voices sang a song about the three little children.

Outside the windows, a fine, drizzly rain was falling. I sneaked up to Hans's room, where I looked at the little dog and wrote on the writing contraption until I was called to go home.

On the way I asked my mother, "How old is Otto?"

"A bit older than you are, pet," she answered, "but remember you must never ask at Uncle Hans's how old Otto is." It seemed to me that the rain suddenly blew a bit harder against us.

I was lost in my thoughts, but I heard my mother add, "They're afraid that Otto won't be taken care of after they're gone." These two bits of information gave me food for days of thought.

Only with the second visit did it become clear to me from the conversation that Otto didn't live there, but at a children's home, and that the woman who brought him was a friend of Aunt Jaanne's who was a nurse at the institution.

It was on a Sunday, and my father went along. When we came in Otto was being talked about in a reprimanding tone. Hans was standing in front of the window and Otto by the antique cabinet with glass doors; Uncle Hans was sitting in a chair beside the table.

"Yes," Aunt Jaanne said, going into the room ahead of us, "we were just talking about Otto."

"Yeah," Otto shouted, "yeah mother!"

"There was a bowl of grapes in the next room, in the office," said Uncle Hans—what he meant was his small study on the street side. "I wondered why he was coming in all the time. And each time he picked off a grape from the bowl, and now they're all gone."

Otto laughed and jumped into the air. His face was glistening with sweat. "Mother doesn't think it's funny at all," Aunt Jaanne said. "You've been very naughty, Otto."

"Otto naughty!" he yelled, his face twisted anxiously.

The phonograph was playing busily most of the time, and the talking grew still more noisy when the Fonteins appeared. I had never seen Mrs. Fontein before, but I had heard at home that whenever she came upon an acquaintance carrying a shopping bag she would hide behind a fence or in a doorway so she wouldn't have to say hello to someone who went out for her own groceries. I had also heard that whenever she was somewhere visiting in the evening she would leave for an hour to go back home and see whether her nineteen-year-old-son had gone to sleep. She was called Aunt Ellie, but grown-ups made fun of her as "crazy Ellie."

Once my mother had gone to see her at home, and she had talked to my mother in the hall, saying that the chiropodist was there; but she had stuffed a gigantic bonbon in my mother's mouth, with the words, "Actually it's one for high society, but I'll let you have it." At home my mother had given only a feeble imitation of her nasal tonsilitis-sufferer's voice, but now I heard the sound unadulterated.

Aunt Ellie's husband, my father, and Uncle Hans went to the study, Uncle Hans propelling himself forward in an extraordinary way, first searching for support with his hands, hunching over, and then letting his frail legs swing forward with a jerk, one after the other.

I followed them through the hall and went into the room behind Uncle Hans. "Was that crazy Ellie there?" I asked Uncle Hans, pointing back in the direction of the living room. Later I comprehended that this question, asked in her husband's presence, must have embarrassed Uncle Hans extremely. He fumbled in his vest pocket till he found a quarter and gave it to me, saying, "You go buy yourself an ice-cream cone."

I went outside just as an ice-cream man was passing. I put the quarter on the cart and said, "An ice-cream cone."

"A five-cent one?" he asked.

"That's all right," I said.

"Or a ten-cent one?"

"That's all right. An ice-cream cone," I said.

"For five cents or ten cents?" he asked then. There was no

definite decision reached, but he made a very large one, and I was taking it from him just as my mother came outside.

"He's been naughty," she said to the man. "He's been begging for it." I kept hold of the ice-cream cone. My mother pulled me along with her. "He still has some change coming!" the ice-cream man called out, but we were already inside and the door banged shut. The ice-cream cone didn't taste good, and I was allowed to put it on a plate in the kitchen.

After that, visits were exchanged regularly. On my birthday my new aunt and uncle gave me a metal toy car that wound up, and I tried not to let them know that I was really too old for it.

Usually they spent New Year's Eve with us, and my father would carry Uncle Hans upstairs with the help of the taxi driver.

Uncle Hans's condition remained the same all those years, but I remember that one afternoon at our place Aunt Jaanne said there was a lameness that had begun in his right arm and came back regularly. It was the same year I started going to a junior high school very near the Boslowitses' apartment. The Sunday before the new school year began I went to see them. I was requested to stay for lunch.

Aunt Jaanne was telling her sister that she had put Hans in a boarding school in Laren, because things couldn't go on the way they were. After the meal, while Uncle Hans was sitting in his study, she said, "When he has a quarrel with his father he puts his hand on the man's head. And that makes him so furious; it's horrible."

She went on to say that a neighbor woman she had talked with that morning over the garden fence had more or less reproached her for the decision, saying, "You already have one boy away from home, and now to send this son away too . . ."

"I've been lying on the sofa all morning crying," said Aunt Jaanne.

"She has her nerve to say that," her sister said. "What business is it of hers?"

I said, "Tomorrow school starts there." I pointed in the direction of the building around the corner. "Do you think I'll get homework the very first day?"

"Well, no, I don't think so," Aunt Jaanne said.

Now that Hans wasn't there I hunted through his room out of curiosity, but I didn't find anything of interest. The little dog was still there, but the writing contraption had disappeared long since.

When Aunt Jaanne came in, I said, "I wanted to borrow a few books," and took up a position in front of the bookcase as though I were deep in reflection. "These." Without thinking, I pulled out two volumes of *Bully and Beanpole,* a children's story about a fat boy and a lean one, and *The Book of Jeremiah Called Michael.* "If Hans doesn't mind," I said.

"If we don't mind," Aunt Jaanne said. "But you're in good standing with us."

"I'll bring them back before long," I said.

Three years before the war the Boslowits family moved to an apartment looking out on the river, a side-canal, and a lot that was being filled in for construction. There was a granite entryway with twenty steps to climb. From there I watched the large-scale aerial-defense exercises that were held one day, I think it was in autumn.

The Boslowitses had invited a large number of people to come and watch, and the younger generation climbed through a window at the head of the stairs above the top-floor neighbors' apartment and onto the roof. Sitting beside the chimney, straddling the ridge, we watched the barrels of the anti-aircraft guns on the vacant sand lot spring back for a shot each time a formation of airplanes passed, a moment before we heard the sound. Fifty yards ahead of us machine-gunners were shooting from the roof of a large mansion set off from the other houses. The Willink boys were there with us, throwing pebbles they had brought along especially for the purpose. Sirens sounded the air-raid alarm and the sky grew overcast. Then new squadrons of airplanes passed over, flying through the cloudlets of the anti-aircraft explosions and discharging green, glowing balls that burned out before they reached the ground. The aerial-defense fire squad spouted water into the canal and the river to test its equipment. At the end of all the turmoil, an amphibian plane landed on the river and skimmed along the surface, then climbed again, over the big bridge connecting the southern and eastern parts of town. I was highly satisfied with the spectacle. Everyone was given tea with crisp, salty crackers.

Half a year later we moved to the center of town, no more than a ten-minute walk from the Boslowits family, on the opposite side of the river. Now we could exchange visits more frequently. Aunt Jaanne came regularly, and on the afternoons when Otto had no school—he was learning paper mat-weaving and bead-stringing somewhere—she would fetch him from the children's home and bring him along to our place for a bit of a change. Walking home from high school one Friday, I saw them approaching from the other direction, Otto hunched over more than ever, springing about like a dancing bear on a chain, so that his mother could hardly hold onto his hand. The eight-year-old neighbor girl from the second floor was jumping rope, and she had fastened one end of the cord to the iron fence around one of the narrow front yards, so she would only have to use one hand to swing the rope. When Otto's mother turned him loose so he could gallop full speed toward our house, the girl purposely stretched out her rope in his path. He stumbled but didn't fall. The girl let go of the rope and fled before Aunt Jaanne, who was so furious she could hardly make a sound.

She went upstairs in a tizzy, right behind Otto, and I followed them. Otto leaped into the hall with a rumble, looking forward to the few old picture postcards my mother gave him each time he came. "That anybody," said Aunt Jaanne, "that anybody could do such a thing—can you understand it? If I had been able to get my hands on her, I would have done I don't know what to her." She grew a bit calmer, but kept on blinking her eyes—a habit I noticed then for the first time.

"Let's go see if we have a postcard for you," my mother said.

"Yeah Aunt Jettie!" Otto forced out, dancing along with her to the cupboard. She dug out three of the cards from a cigar box. He sniffed at them and jumped in the air.

"Be careful, boy. There are people living downstairs," my mother said.

"Where's Otto going?" asked Aunt Jaanne.

"Yeah yeah mother!"

"Where are you going?"

"Yeah mother!"

"No, Otto, you know well enough. Where are you going?" When Otto had still not given a satisfactory answer, she said, "To Russia."

"To Russia yeah mother!" Otto shouted.

"You see, Jettie," said Aunt Jaanne, "a professor in Russia has completely cured a number of children with an operation. And ever since then, he's going to Russia." Another bit of news had to do with Uncle Hans's condition. He had collapsed and was in bed, and his right arm was paralyzed almost all the time. "And besides that there's his temper," she said. "That's something terrible."

As a more encouraging bit of information, she told us that a doctor who had treated Uncle Hans ten years before had come to visit and had said, "Man, I thought you'd died a long time ago."

That wasn't all the news. They were thinking of buying a new wheelchair for Uncle Hans so that when he had got a bit better he would be able to be outside in the air more and could go visiting here and there without it costing so much.

"But he doesn't want to," said Aunt Jaanne, "because he thinks he'll seem like an invalid then."

"But that's what he is," my mother said.

Uncle Hans did get his wheelchair, despite his opposition, but not until quite a while later. It was a three-wheeled one, propelled by levers that turned the front wheel and guided the vehicle at the same time. It had to be taken from a garage each time, and then Uncle Hans had to be carried down the high stone entryway. He hadn't had the wheelchair long before they rented a ground floor apartment. It was in the street behind ours. Though it was a dark, dank house, there were advantages to it, since the Block Committee agreed to having the wheelchair stand in the entry, and a friend who was a carpenter made a letter box in a windowpane in Uncle Hans's study so the postman could drop his letters practically on his desk. Going out in the wheelchair was an act of his own in appearance only, for someone had to push him—his thin hands, and especially the right one, had no strength at all.

One Sunday afternoon we—my parents and I—were coming back from a birthday party together with Otto, Aunt Jaanne, and Uncle Hans, and I was patiently pushing the wheelchair. We were crossing a bridge that sloped rather steeply. On the other side of the canal we had to turn left. On the downslope the wheelchair began to go faster and faster; I held it back, but Uncle Hans ordered me to let loose. I obeyed. There was an intersection just beyond the bridge, and the presence of a traffic policeman made it impossible to turn left right away. Vehicles had to wait for the traffic signal, then cross over and line up on the right side of the street.

But Uncle Hans zoomed down the bridge and cut diagonally around the corner without waiting. "You can't do that," I called after him. Right behind the traffic policeman he veered left, but his speed and the incline made the wheelchair topple over and hit the street with a bang. The policeman and some pedestrians came hurrying up and set the wheelchair upright, with Uncle Hans still in it. He hadn't been hurt at all, but he said nothing, and even after we got to the Boslowitses he sat at the table in silence, staring straight ahead.

Aunt Jaanne comforted Otto, because she thought he had seen the fall and was frightened by it. "It wasn't father that tipped over, but someone else, wasn't it, Otto; it was some other man, not father."

"Not father!" Otto shouted, and he leaned his elbow on a teacup, which broke. It was a gray day with no rain falling, though a still sky constantly threatened it.

On my sixteenth birthday, that same spring, Hans came along with Aunt Jaanne and Uncle Hans to visit. His mother had decided to have him come back home. "If there's going to be a war, I'd rather have him at home," she said. He was to be a salesman in an uncle's business.

"You say if there's going to be a war, as if there's nothing going on now," my father said. At that my interest in the conversation was aroused. It was true that England and France were at war with Germany, but to my dissatisfaction there had not been any military activities of importance to follow.

From time to time I went to the movies with Joost, the younger of the two Willink boys, and before the main feature there would be some insignificant news shots from the front, with camouflaged cannon standing ready or firing a shot every quarter of an hour. Once there was a favorable exception to this monotony in some shots of the grounded German battleship *Graf von Spee*, beautifully unraveled and shattered. "Horrors of the war, nice," Joost said in a comical tone as a shot from the air gave a last view of the wreckage.

"What I'd like best is short, violent street fighting here in town," I said. "From window to window, with hand grenades and white flags. But not for more than two days, because then it would be boring again."

One evening in May when I went to ask if we could borrow an electric toaster from the Boslowitses, I found Uncle

Hans, Aunt Jaanne, and Hans together in the twilight. There was a neighbor visiting them. They were so deep in conversation that they didn't notice it right away when I came in. "That means something," the neighbor said. "I say that has a significance. It means a lot more than we know." Confused, I stood waiting in the door to the sitting room for a little bit, till Aunt Jaanne caught sight of me.

"Oh, it's you," she said. "Have you heard that the furloughs are all canceled? This man's son has to be back this evening already, and be in the barracks tonight."

"No," I said, "is that so?"

"That's what they said over the radio," the neighbor said.

"Then there's something in the air anyway," I said, and I felt a deep emotion rising inside me. That same week, on Thursday night, almost everyone in the neighborhood appeared in the streets a few hours after midnight. Airplanes went droning over, anti-aircraft thundered, and searchlights pushed their shafts upward between the thin tufts of clouds.

"They're getting something to put up with again over in England," said a milkman who had concluded that they were German planes on their way to English cities and being shot at over Dutch territory by our neutral military forces. He proved to be right about the nationality of the planes, but the rest of his hypothesis was refuted when we came to realize the meaning of the deep thuds and flashes of light on the southwest horizon.

A little after seven o'clock Aunt Jaanne came upstairs. I wasn't there at the time, because the Willink boys and their sister had come for me. I had gone along to their house, and from the balcony I could see black clouds of smoke hovering above a spot that couldn't be anything but Schiphol Airport.

"It's war," said the Willink girl, whose name was Lies. We went back to my house together, elated at so many thrilling events all at one time. It was a quarter to eight.

"It's war," said my mother. "It's been on the radio already."

"What did they say exactly?" I asked.

"Oh, I can't repeat it all, you should have listened yourself," she answered.

Aunt Jaanne sat in the easy chair with a black velvet cap on her head, blinking her eyes. The radio was dead, and we sat waiting impatiently for the beginning of the regular broadcasting day at eight o'clock. It was the custom to introduce the day's broadcasts with a rooster's crow.

"I wonder if they'll do cock-a-doodle-doo the same as usual this morning," said my father, coming in from the hall.

I fervently hoped that the rumors flying through the neighborhood were all true. "Really at war, wonderful," I said to myself softly.

The radio clock began the soft poise it makes before it strikes. After the sixteen notes of the chime, it struck, slow and clear. Then the rooster crowed. "That's really a shame!" said my father.

I was frightened, because everything could still be spoilt. This was probably proof that war hadn't broken out at all. I was put at ease only when it was announced that the borders of Holland, Belgium, and Luxembourg had been crossed by German troops.

I went to school that morning content, while Aunt Jaanne still sat staring straight ahead without saying a word.

At school a solemn mood prevailed. The building was

to be used as a hospital, and the headmaster made an announcement of the fact in the auditorium. After that we all sang the national anthem. The fact that the school was closed for the time being made the day still lighter, as though all things had been made new.

We didn't see Aunt Jaanne again until the next Tuesday afternoon. She came to visit us alone, and she looked pale. "What are you doing?" she asked. "What a smell—is there something burning? Things look pretty bad."

"Pretty bad," my mother said. "They've just capitulated."

We had begun burning books and pamphlets in the stove, and it puffed and smoked from being stuffed overfull. At the same time my brother and my father were busy filling two burlap bags and a suitcase with books. After dark they threw them in the canal.

Everywhere in the neighborhood fires glowed that evening, with new loads of things to be burned being carried up constantly, sometimes chestsful at a time. Many other people threw everything in the canals. Sometimes, in the general haste, this or that was left lying on the edge. Wandering along the canal in the twilight, I found a book with a flaming red cover—I have forgotten the title—that my mother later took out of my room and refused to give back.

After the announcement of the capitulation, Aunt Jaanne let it be repeated to her once more and then suddenly went away. The following day brought two interesting events. Toward noon the first Germans rode into the city. They were men on motorcycles, dressed in spotless green capes. A few people stood along the road to watch them crossing the bridge. Aunt Jaanne had seen them, too, and when she came to see us Wednesday evening she called them "frogs."

I wasn't at home, because I was busy. Hundreds of fish had come swimming to the surface of the canals, gulping for air—it was said because salt water had been let into the canals by mistake. I was catching those in front of the house with a big fishnet; they made no attempt to escape, and I took home a pail full of them.

The next day school began again, and the very first evening I went seeking consolation at a small movie-house where that week, for the last time, there was still a French film. The movie, *Hôtel du Nord,* was about a suicide pact in which the boy succeeded in shooting the girl, then lacked the courage to turn his gun on himself. But the girl recovered, and it all ended with a reconciliation between them and an acceptance of life when she came to meet him at the prison after he had served his sentence. I felt satisfied with the way the problem was solved.

At home I found Aunt Jaanne sitting on the sofa and my mother pouring coffee.

It was growing dark in the room, because the lights hadn't been turned on yet. Unrolling the blackout paper and fastening it with thumbtacks was a cumbersome job. And so I found them sitting by the pensive light of the tea warmer.

"You have to blackout," I said. "That light shines outside."

"You do it then, will you?" said my mother.

I remember that one window was ajar when I let down the roll of paper. "Hans sent a letter to an aunt in Berlin, quite a while ago," Aunt Jaanne said. "It just came back, undeliverable. Moved, destination unknown, it said on it."

Just then a gust of wind lifted the blackout paper and the

curtain for a few seconds, chasing a piece of paper off the table. I shut the window quickly.

Late one afternoon when there was no school I dropped by the Boslowitses. It was high summer, and Uncle Hans was sitting in front of his office window in the sun. Almost immediately he turned the conversation to his sickness and a doctor called Witvis, who had already been there several times and wanted to try something new to cure him. "He'll have to make me run like a rabbit," he said. "You'd like to have a cigarette, wouldn't you?" he asked, and got up to look for the box. "Tell me where they are and I'll get them," I said, but he shuffled to the corner of the room and took a flat, square copper box from a table. "Are you laughing?" he asked, his back turned toward me. "No, honest," I said.

Hans came in and sat down on his father's desk. "How's it going?" I asked. "That selling, do you like it?"

"Today my turnover was close to a thousand guilders," he answered.

"Is there any news?" asked Aunt Jaanne.

"News that the Germans are advancing on Brest," I answered. "They're making a terrific hullabaloo on the radio." Then I told them what a fat boy in my class had claimed. According to a prediction made by a French priest forty years before, the Germans were to be defeated near Orléans. "He also wrote that the city on the Meuse will be destroyed," I said.

Aunt Jaanne said, "If you'll bring me the book that says that, I'll give you something."

That same afternoon, not long before dinner, I went to the Willinks for a little while to tell them the latest news from the radio. Just after I sat down in Eric's room the anti-aircraft artillery began popping restlessly. Two airplanes glistened in the sunlight, flying so high it was impossible to make out their forms, but only a glittering reflection.

A bit later we heard the rattle of machine guns and the terrifying sound of a fighter plane zooming by close over-head. From time to time when the noise grew too strong, we would hurry inside from the balcony; we could also hear the rattling of the plane's guns.

Then it was still for a moment, and we saw a black swath through the sky with a flaming star dropping rapidly at its point. The light was white, like the light of an acetylene torch. Then we saw a second column of smoke beside the flame: the plane had broken in two.

After a moment it all disappeared behind the houses. There were no parachutes to be seen anywhere in the sky. "May God guard those who fare on the sea and in the sky," I said solemnly. No air-raid alarm had been given.

After dinner Hans Boslowits came to our house. "Do you know what kind of a plane it was that came down?" he asked.

"No, I don't know," I said.

"It was German," he declared.

"How do you know?" I asked. "Have you already heard where it came down?"

"Look," Hans said, polishing his glasses with his hand-kerchief, "we have our sources of information."

"I hope it's so," I said, "but I don't believe anyone can know anything for sure yet."

"We have our sources of information," he said, and went away.

The next day, I'm certain it was a weekday, on my way

home from the movies in the afternoon I saw the announcement of the French surrender being posted as a bulletin in front of a newspaper office. When I gave a report at home, my mother said, "Then they're asking for an armistice. That's not the same thing. Go to Aunt Jaanne's and tell her exactly what it said."

"It may be propaganda," Aunt Jaanne said, but I could tell she didn't doubt the announcement for an instant. That same evening she came to our place, and it was then that she told us what had happened to her all of four weeks earlier.

One afternoon two Germans in uniform had come in an automobile. "Put your hands up," one of them had said on entering Uncle Hans's room. "Don't be witty, mister," he had answered in German, "I can't even stand on my legs."

They had searched the apartment and then declared that he had to go along. Uncle Hans had gone to get dressed; once they saw him dragging himself through the house, his crippled state became so completely obvious they must have realized the foolishness of making an arrest. Then they watched Aunt Jaanne fasten a rubber flask for urinating onto his waist. "They asked if I was the only one who could do that," she went on. "I said I was the only one. Then they wrote down some more and went away again. It wasn't very pleasant though." She blinked her eyes, and a few slight quivers shot through the muscles of her face.

"How is Uncle Hans, anyway?" my mother asked.

"He's not getting any worse," Aunt Jaanne said. "Just now he's able to use that hand to write with again."

"That's something," said my mother.

Summer and fall went drably by. It was after New Year's, dull, damp spring-like weather. The second Sunday in the new year the parents of my classmate Jim had asked me to dinner, and unexpectedly I ran into Hans there. Jim's father was a wholesale dealer in veal and had an amazingly fat belly, but he took things lightly and was a lot of fun. Although he had had three stomach operations, he didn't allow it to restrict him in any way.

"I like everything, so long as there aren't any pins in it," he said at the table. As a gesture of friendliness they had also invited my parents, whom they didn't know.

"I don't read German books anymore," said a small gray-haired man when the conversation was on literature for a moment. At once the talk turned to the war and surmises of how long it would last.

"Now I'd say half a year at the most," said Jim's father. "But actually he's not going to hold out that long."

"The way it's going now, it could last twenty-five years," my father said, smiling.

Hans, who proved to know one of Jim's brothers, had his guitar with him, and he played a renowned tune, *Skating on the Rainbow*, with a great deal of violence. When talk of the war came up, he said, "It's going to be over this year."

"What makes you think so, Hans?" asked my mother.

He answered, "The circles who keep me informed know very well, Aunt Jettie—I repeat, very well—what's going on."

Five or six weeks later Aunt Jaanne climbed the steps to our apartment, visibly upset. "The greenies are catching the boys all around Waterlooplein," she said. "Can Simon go check for me? No, he had better go to Hans's office and tell him he can't go out on the streets. But wait, I'll call him. Have Simon wait."

"First come and sit down," my mother said. It was a Wednesday afternoon. We succeeded in calming Aunt Jaanne, "Now go call up Hans," my mother said.

"I already have," she said.

"Oh, have you?" my mother said.

"I'm going out there to have a look," I declared.

"You'll be careful, won't you?" asked my mother.

I cycled quickly to the neighborhood around Waterlooplein and brought back a detailed report on everything. Uncle Hans puffed slowly on his stubby black pipe. "You've got on a nice sweater there," he said in the middle of my account. "Is it new?"

Aunt Jaanne was constantly telephoning the office where Hans worked. He was to stay there at night; I heard her promise to take him bedding and food. At her request I took the telephone. "Don't believe that what you're going to say will be of the slightest importance, high and mighty Simon," said the voice on the other end.

"Is that so," I answered, smiling, because Aunt Jaanne was keeping a close eye on me.

"That woman sure nags a lot," he went on. "Just tell her for me that she's a horrible old nag."

The receiver had a very clear tone, so I drummed on the floor with my left foot. "Yes, that's right," I said loudly. "I can imagine that. Fine."

"What do you mean?" he asked.

"That's it exactly," I said, "that in any case you'll be careful—but you are, so I hear. Good-bye. See you." And I put down the receiver, even though Hans had suddenly begun to shout so loudly that the telephone emitted squeaking sounds.

"Well, what did he say?" asked Aunt Jaanne.

"He says," I replied, "that we are all nervous and say crazy things to each other. But you shouldn't be at all worried, he says. Of course he'll stay inside. He says in a day everything will be over."

"You can talk on the telephone again," said Aunt Jaanne, satisfied. Then she looked out of the window and said, "Don't be worried: it's a nice theory."

Four days later Aunt Jaanne came to see my mother, who was at some friends' somewhere and might be back any moment. While Aunt Jaanne sat waiting for her, the fat magician who lived around the corner also came up the stairs. On the steps he always whistled the melody that preceded broadcasts from London. "You shouldn't whistle like that on the stairs," I said. "You don't get anywhere by it, and it's dangerous."

After he had listened to what meager news there was, he said, "I think they're going to lose, only I don't know whether it'll be before I'm dead and buried or after." He shook with laughter and went away, whistling the melody loudly on the stairs. He had barely gone when my mother came home.

Only then did Aunt Jaanne say, "Parkman's daughter is dead." She explained how the daughter and son-in-law of a neighbor across the street from her had swallowed poison together. The man had been revived in the hospital and was recovering. "He's screaming, and they have to hold him down," Aunt Jaanne said. Whom did she mean, I thought, the father or the husband?

June was very mild, a bright, sunny early summer month.

One afternoon while my mother was sitting in front of the open window knitting, Aunt Jaanne came in with Otto. She looked pale, and the skin of her face was cracked and chalky, though she didn't use powder. "Mother mother," Otto called impatiently.

"Be quiet a little, dear, that's a sweet boy," said Aunt Jaanne.

She had to tell about something that had happened to a nephew of hers. Cycling through the heart of town, he had violated a traffic regulation and was stopped by a man in black boots, partly uniformed, partly in civilian dress. The man had grinned as he wrote down the name.

One evening a few days afterward, a nondescript man in dark-colored clothes came to the door. He said that the nephew had to appear at an office somewhere in the center of town the next afternoon because of a traffic violation—in order, so he said, to settle the affair.

The boy went, but his mother went along. At the entrance to the office she was held back, but her son was allowed to enter. After twenty minutes he came stumbling outside, vomiting. There were several welts and bleeding gashes on his face and dirt on his clothes as though they had been dragged across the floor.

For a high fee, the two of them took a cab with rubber tires and a pony to pull it. When they got home the doctor found a slight brain concussion and a contusion of the left shoulder blade, and the collarbone on the same side was broken.

They had let him wait in a little room. The man who had stopped him on the street came in first, then he called in some others, some of them carrying billy clubs. "This is a sassy kid that called me bastard," he explained. One of the others struck the boy under the chin and then all six or seven of them began hitting and kicking him.

"It started all at once," he had told Aunt Jaanne. One man with greasy hair kept trying to kick him in the groin. He stumbled in his attempt to avoid the man's blows and ended up lying on his back. Before he could take up a safer position, one of the men stamped on his chest. After he had turned over, someone, he thought the gray-haired man, stood on his back.

Then a bell rang or a whistle blew, in any case there was a shrill sound that made everybody stop; after that he heard all kinds of voices, but he couldn't remember anything about what happened from then on until he came outside.

"You know that Joseph's people got notice of his death?" said Aunt Jaanne.

"No," my mother said, "I didn't know."

"But they had a letter from him from camp, too, with a lot later date," Aunt Jaanne went on, "but now they don't hear any more news."

They fell silent. Aunt Jaanne looked at Otto and said, "The doctor has given him some powders. He's stayed dry for two nights already, I heard from the nurse." My mother remembered that she had neglected to give Otto any picture postcards, and she hunted out two of them from the cupboard; one was in bright colors, a view of some foreign city with a pink sky.

When I went to see Hans Boslowits one evening several weeks later, he was playing his guitar. He would slap the strings with his open hand and beat up and down with his foot. At my request he played *O Joseph, Joseph*, but I wasn't pleased by the performance because he followed the melody by singing "ta ta ta ta" with too much emphasis, tilting his head up so that his throat was foolishly tensed.

"It's the heartbeat of our society, this music," he said. At that moment someone tapped on the panel of the living-room door. The visitor had already entered the hall; he called out his name loudly and Aunt Jaanne answered, "Yes, come on in, neighbor."

"Mrs. Boslowits," said the neighbor, entering, "I don't suppose you've heard yet that Dr. Witvis is dead?"

"How can that be?" Aunt Jaanne asked.

"I only heard it just now," he said. "It happened last night."

Late in the evening, he went on, the doctor had taken a razor and slashed both his two small sons' wrists, holding their forearms in a basin of warm water while he did it because that prevented pain. After his wife had opened the artery on her wrist herself, he cut his the same way. The order of events was deduced from the position of the victims and the presence of a second razor in his wife's hand. The mother and the children were already dead when they were found, and the father was unconscious. He was given a blood transfusion in the hospital after the wound had been closed, but he died before noon without having regained consciousness.

When I went to the Boslowitses to borrow half a loaf of bread one Sunday afternoon late in the fall, I found Otto beside the phonograph.

"Otto is going on a trip," Aunt Jaanne said. "Isn't that right, Otto?"

"Yeah mother," he called, "Otto on trip!"

"Where in the world is he going to?" I asked.

Aunt Jaanne's face gave the impression of being inflamed by fever. "He can't stay at the children's home or the school anymore," she answered. "He has to go to Apeldoorn. I'm taking him there tomorrow."

I saw only then that the sliding doors to the back room stood open, and Uncle Hans lay there in bed. The bedstead had white iron rods, with copper globes at the four corners. The sick man's face was thin, but even so it looked swollen, as though it was moist inside.

On a chair were bottles of medicine, a breakfast plate with a knife, and a chessboard. "I was playing chess with Hans this afternoon," he said, "but Otto kept tipping it over."

He kept to his bed the following days as well, and his situation turned serious. Winter was coming, and the new doctor said that the rooms should be kept quite warm. For a long time Uncle Hans could still go to the bathroom by himself, but eventually he had to be helped.

"He's so awfully heavy I can't do it," Aunt Jaanne said. "Actually he doesn't even cooperate."

After New Year's the doctor strongly recommended his being admitted to a hospital, and he was taken there early that same week.

"He's in really good hands," Aunt Jaanne told my mother after a visit. The doctors and the nurses are all so nice."

"He doesn't have any notion of things anymore," she went on soon after that. "I don't understand what's going on inside him nowadays. Hans took him some oranges—he could buy them from someone at the office. He says, father, these cost sixty cents apiece, be sure you eat them. But he didn't eat a single one; he gave them all away. Of course you should share things, but this is enough to make you furious."

"From tomorrow on we have to be inside at eight o'clock," Aunt Jaanne said to my mother one day late in the spring. "Will you go for the evening visiting hours? I can't get back in time and what good does it do Hans if I have to go away again after three minutes? I'll just stay a little longer in the daytime then; they won't mind that."

"He looks good, he's getting fat," my mother said after she had been to visit the first time, reporting to Aunt Jaanne at her place the same evening. But Aunt Jaanne was not much interested. Hans wasn't home yet, and she asked my mother to go somewhere and call his office, because their telephone had just been taken away.

"Have Simon go to the office and see if he's still there." My mother was just about to carry out her request when Hans came in. The streets had been cordoned off, and they had been warned at the office. He waited till everything seemed quiet again, but halfway home he had had to take refuge in a public toilet. Finally eight o'clock had come and he had finished the last section, through our neighborhood, on the run.

"We aren't allowed to leave the city anymore," Aunt Jaanne said one night when I came to tell her that my mother couldn't visit Uncle Hans the next Friday evening. "Ask your mother if she'll go see Otto this week."

The next day, a Wednesday afternoon, Aunt Jaanne came to our home. "They're taking inventory," she said. After my mother had asked her to sit down and had poured her a cup of apple tea, she said that the inventory takers had been at all the neighbors' in her building—two men, each with a briefcase. They had inspected everything and noted it all down.

They had found the first-floor neighbors' five-year-old son playing with a little dark red toy purse on the stairs. One of the two men took it away from him, opened it, and fished out a nickel five-cent piece and three small silver pieces, then gave it back. "That one isn't a quarter," the child said. "It's a coin from the old days, my father said."

"You just be very quiet, little boy," the man had said then. "Very quiet."

It was impossible to determine whether or not she had heard the knock on her door; at any rate they had disappeared without visiting her apartment.

She asked me to go along with her right away, and she had me pack a Frisian clock, some antique pottery, two carved ivory candlesticks, and the two wall tiles into a suitcase and take them with me. I carried them to our house and made two more trips to get old china plates, a camera, and a small, delicate mirror.

Every other week, usually on a Tuesday, my mother went to visit Otto in the big institution at Apeldoorn. The first time, Aunt Jaanne sat at our place in the afternoon waiting for her to come back. "How was it?" she asked my mother. "He looks fine," my mother answered, "and he was really glad to see me. The nurses are all very kind to him."

"Didn't he ask about home?" asked Aunt Jaanne.

"No, not at all," my mother said, "and he was having fun playing with the other children. When I went away he looked sad for a moment, but that he misses anything really—no, you couldn't say that."

She gave Aunt Jaanne a detailed description of how she was received by the nurse in charge of the ward and how she had given the fruit and cookies and candy to be handed out. But one part, a bag of cherries, she had given to Otto himself when they went walking in the sun along the path in the woods.

"I kept feeding him a few at a time," she said. "But he wanted to take them out of the bag himself. I was afraid he'd slobber juice on his clothes, but it wasn't so bad." Later, after Aunt Jaanne had gone, she told me that he was sloppily dressed, with his shorts held up by a rope instead of suspenders or a belt. "And his shoes," she said. "I don't see how they can fit onto his feet in such a crazy way. There's not enough staff, but the people do their best."

She also told me that Otto had said several times, "To mother."

"Mother is at home; she'll come some other time," she had answered.

"Mother home," he had yelled out then. He had cried when she went away late in the afternoon.

A week later Aunt Jaanne came to our house one evening just after supper. "They're starting to come after them," she said. "They're coming and getting them. No more summonses, they just come and get them. They came and got the Allegro family. Do you know them?"

"No, I don't know them," my mother said.

Aunt Jaanne wanted me to go to the hospital right away and ask for a paper certifying that Uncle Hans was seriously ill. I went, and at the main entrance I was directed to one of the wings, where I handed over my note at an office. After ten minutes I was presented a white sealed envelope and took it home to Aunt Jaanne.

The next evening she appeared for a second time. She asked me if I would go again. "It says in it that he's seriously ill; that should be mortally ill," she said.

"I don't know if they'll put that in," I answered, "but we'll see."

After the head nurse had taken Aunt Jaanne's note and the first certificate, I waited a quarter of an hour and was given a new letter.

"Do you know what, Simon," Aunt Jaanne said two evenings later. "You'll have to go one more time and ask if they can make a whole new paper giving the nature of the illness in it. The nature of the illness. And not in Latin; if it has to be, in German, but at any rate so it's understandable."

She gave me back the last certificate, but without any accompanying note. I set off for the hospital again.

"Mrs. Boslowits asks if the nature of the illness can be given in it," I said. "And it's better if it's not in Latin." The head nurse took the envelope and came back a little later.

"Will you wait a bit?" she asked. After some time I received a sealed envelope, exactly the same as the others.

I went at once to deliver it, and I found Aunt Jaanne and Hans both sitting in front of the bay window. The room was almost completely dark. The draperies were open and the curtain pushed aside, so they could see the street from the window.

"Look, that's nice," Aunt Jaanne said when she read the paper.

"Did you think that would do any good?" Hans asked.

"Of course," I answered. "He knows, he knows," I said.
"What are you saying?" asked Aunt Jaanne.
"I was humming," I said.

Not only my mother but other friends of the Boslowits family who dropped by in the evenings spoke about the situation in gloomy wonderment. "It's just like a haunted house," my mother said.

I went there regularly in the evenings, and everything was always the same. I would ring the bell, the apartment door would be unlocked, and by the time I entered the hall, Aunt Jaanne would already be back inside. When I came into the living room, Aunt Jaanne would be sitting to the left in the bay window and Hans to the right. Once I was inside Aunt Jaanne would leave her post again for a moment to scurry into the hall and lock the door. When I went away they would follow me and lock the door after me, and by the time I was in the street I could see them already sitting like statues in front of the window again. Then I would make a waving motion, but they never reacted.

One Tuesday morning some neighbors of theirs came to tell us that about half past eight the night before two policemen with black helmets had come. Aunt Jaanne had shown them the certificate from the hospital, and one of them threw the beam of a flashlight on it. "Who are you?" he had asked Hans. When he had identified himself, the other man said, "He's not on the list." "Both of you have to come with us," the first one had said then.

Uncle Hans said nothing when he heard the news. They thought he hadn't heard or hadn't really understood, and they repeated it emphatically several times. He tried to raise himself up, and after they had put a pillow behind his back he sat looking out of the window. Finally the visitors, a friend of Aunt Jaanne's and her daughter, went home again.

One day some time later a neighbor came to visit. "They are emptying the Invalide," she said. She had watched while hundreds of very old people were carried down the stairs and out of the building to vehicles standing ready for them. One ninety-two-year-old man whom she thought she had known once had called out, "They're waiting on me hand and foot."

"The Apeldoorn Woods were emptied yesterday too," she said.

"What did you say about Otto?" I asked my mother when she came back from her next visit to Uncle Hans.

"The truth—that everything was taken away," she said. "He only hopes he's put to death right away. The doctors and nurses stayed with the patients, did you know that?"

"No," I said, "I didn't know."

Early the following week a friend of Uncle Hans's hired a cab and took him from the hospital to an attic room he had been able to arrange for him at some friends' in the center of town. Late that night he also took the wheelchair—the tires had already been stolen from it—from the entryway of Uncle Hans's house. It was only four days until everything in the apartment was taken away, but it was agreed not to tell Uncle Hans for the time being.

He lay there all alone in his new location, but a nurse came twice a day to look after him. Only a few people knew where he was.

During the summer everything went as well as could be hoped for. But when fall came, another hiding place for

Uncle Hans had to be found, because a stove couldn't be used in his room.

They succeeded in obtaining a place for him in an old people's home. The papers would be taken care of.

When he was told the decision, he showed his disappointment. He explained he would rather be taken in by friends.

Sometimes he didn't seem to know what he was saying; one afternoon he said to the nurse, "Do you still remember when I was twenty-seven? No, I mean 1927. I know exactly what I mean, so—" and after that he lay lost in thought.

One Wednesday a friend, a woman who was an artist, was visiting him. "You like that atlas a lot, don't you?" he asked. "Tell me the truth, now." He had an atlas of the world that was supposed to be very extensive and valuable, and friends had been able to rescue it from his apartment.

When the nurse came that afternoon, he said, "Take that atlas along. I've given it to Ali."

"What nonsense," she said, "it's much too nice to give away."

"Take it along, I said." Then he asked for something to drink.

The following day the daughter of Aunt Jaanne's friend came and found him asleep. "He's sleeping," she said at home. In the evening the nurse came again, found him resting, took his pulse, and left satisfied. The next morning she came back at the usual time and found his body already cold. She lifted up the head; its little tuft of hair felt damp to the touch. The thin mouth was closed, and the glasses gave the face an unreal expression.

"I didn't understand it all right away," she said later. "And I thought I heard something strange, but it was a carpet sweeper on the ground floor."

When she saw the empty box beside the glass of water, she began to comprehend. But she figured out that it couldn't have contained more than four sleeping pills. The only conclusion was that he had regularly saved one at a time and so built up a supply.

That night the friend who had taken him out of the hospital and the man who had given up the room for him together carried the body downstairs and, without splashing, lowered it on a rope into the canal beside the house; it sank immediately, so I was told.

They both hurried back inside the house and waited together with the nurse until they could go home at four in the morning.

In the meantime they discussed all things: the distances of planets, the duration of the war, the existence of a god. The two men were also given a bit of information by the nurse: she was able to tell them that Uncle Hans's money could have served to maintain him for at least another year.

"So that wasn't the reason," she said.

Translated by James S Holmes and Hans van Marle

The Return
Marga Minco

HE COULD NOT GET TO SLEEP. He had been awake for hours. It was warm. He carefully pushed the blankets aside, making sure Rosa did not notice anything. She slept with her arm on the cover. A reddish arm. He had warned her not to stay out in the sun too long. That always made her laugh. "My skin isn't as delicate as yours." During their time in hiding they had hardly seen the sun. They stayed in a tiny attic room on a farm, with only one small window, up high in the wall, made intransparent with white chalk. It was carefully blacked out in the evening. A few times a day he climbed on a chair to look outside. With his fingernail he had scratched a small peephole in the chalk, about the size of a penny. You could look out over the barnyard to a stretch of country road, a wide curve, lined with poplars.

"A woman is passing by," he told Rosa. "She is about thirty. A boy on a bicycle. With big ears. A haycart. They are going to milk the cows. Two kids on a vegetable crate." It had become a routine game. You could kill time with it. Sometimes he would stand motionless at his lookout, with baited breath. A dark DKW screeched around the curve. A truck full of soldiers appeared, a whole column. The walls shook. Once two soldiers entered the yard, to refill their canteens. He did not move and did not say a word. Rosa, seated with a book on her lap, looked up at him. She held the page she meant to turn over between her fingers. It lasted about five minutes, but days later they could still see it in each other's eyes.

A big fly buzzed over the bed, just above his head. He did not want to swat at it, afraid of waking Rosa. Now the fly was sitting on the screen. He saw the dark speck crawl over the mesh and fly away, when a ray of light came in from below. It must have come from the neighbor's yard, from the shed. He heard footsteps, a door squeaked, something was being moved. The man often worked in the shed. Probably a handyman, someone with a hobby. What exactly he was doing, he did not know. They had been neighbors only for a short time. Rosa was sorry that the former neighbors had left. She liked the little children, who played in the yard and whom she called inside when the weather turned bad. When the new occupants arrived the first thing she said was: "They don't have any children." The moving van came from The Hague. City folk. People from the big city don't bother with their neighbors. They are not used to it. Rosa stirred for a second. The big bright spot in the room bothered him. But when he closed the curtain, it became too stuffy.

The day it was safe to go outside again it had been stifling hot in their hiding place. The window wouldn't open. They heard the farmer's wife running through the hallway, up the steps, calling. Suddenly, she stood in the middle of the room. "Come outside," she yelled, "come out, come outside!" Rosa dropped a cup on the floor. She covered her face with her hands. "It can't be true," she said. "What can't be true? What is it?" he asked. He was cold and trembling.

"The Germans are capitulating. I just heard. It really is true. Come outside with me, hurry!" Of course they knew of the advance of the allied troops. They knew it could be all over any day.

But now that it had finally happened, he was shocked. What to do next? He wanted to go outside, and yet he didn't want to. They walked down the street with small stiff steps. The war was over; you could tell by the flags hanging out of the windows and the people wearing orange and red, white, and blue. A boy came by, playing a trumpet that was completely out of tune. His face was purple. A farmer's cart filled with cheering children followed them. As they shivered in the warm sun, they walked arm in arm along the road to the village, their eyes blinking.

"Here we go," he said, outside again. "We can come and go as we please." He listened to his own voice. It felt as if he hadn't spoken out loud in years.

"Where are we going?" asked Rosa.

"Just for a walk."

"Let's have a look at the village. Have we ever been here?"

"Not as far as I know."

"The scenery is supposed to be beautiful."

"Yes, so it seems."

They had lived here two and a half years without seeing any of it. They arrived one winter evening, after a long train ride. They felt uncomfortable in the train compartment with their false IDs and their silent companions. They were the only people to get off at the small station. He had not been able to make out the name of the town. It had still been a half hour walk to the farm, over dark country roads. They had to hold each other by the hand.

"It's just like we're on vacation," said Rosa. She had become thin. Her skin was pallid. Broad gray streaks ran through her dark hair. Her shoulders hunched forward. He had never noticed that about her before.

They passed by an office supply store. Rosa stopped. Someone had constructed a pyramid of paper string on a faded piece of cardboard. It was decorated with little orange flags and surrounded by pictures of the royal family. But she looked at the postcards in the front. Faded cards from long before the war, displaying an unreal tranquility.

"Look how beautiful it is around here." She stretched to look at the postcards in the top row.

"Why don't you buy some?"

"Shall I buy a little packet? How many are there in a packet?"

"About a dozen, I think."

"To send, you mean."

He did not answer.

"To whom, to whom would we send them?"

"It is for you. A keepsake."

While she was in the store he waited in front of the window. He saw his reflection in the glass. An old man, in an ill-fitting suit. It had become far too big for him. A man with thin hair, bags under his eyes, tired of doing nothing, of waiting. He stretched and took a deep breath. His head stuck out a little farther from the roomy collar. He pulled his shoulders back, stretched his arms downward, and planted his feet solidly on the ground, until he felt his whole body tense up and his bones creak.

"Are you doing exercises?" Rosa came out of the store.

"A little, yes. I need it. It has been a long time."

"Two and a half years."

"It feels like three times that long."

She put the packet of postcards in her purse. "But it's all over now, isn't it?" Her hand touched his sleeve slightly.

"Come, let's sit down in a terrace café somewhere, in the sun."

"If they have something to drink."

"Here they still might. Surrogate coffee and surrogate lemonade, it doesn't matter. It's the thought that counts."

"Yes, it is legal again, isn't it?"

They walked slowly, in search of an outdoor café. He felt as if there was something he had known for a long time, that he was certain of now, but that had not yet dawned on Rosa. Or was she just pretending? Didn't she want to let on that she suspected the same? That it wasn't really over. That, in fact, it had only just begun for them.

The fly sat still somewhere. Maybe on the side of the bed. Downstairs the light was still on. There was a scraping noise, as if someone were using a file. He was right: the time ahead was more difficult to cope with than the years in hiding. The days they didn't dare to talk to each other, when they were hesitant to use certain words. Many words now had a double meaning for them. The neighbor dropped something on the tile floor. Of course he had a workbench in the shed. Who knows, his wife probably did not like him to spend his days puttering, and that was why he did it at night, while she was asleep.

They had stayed in the village a few more weeks. They could not find transportation back to their own home that readily. Instead, they moved into another room on the farm, where the people did everything to make them feel more comfortable. But he was more in a hurry to get away than Rosa. Every day he went into the village to see if it was possible to make a telephone call yet, or if the mail was operating again, or if he could send a telegram. The man at the window said the same thing every time: "Sir, you'll have to be patient just a little longer. They are working very hard to get everything going again." He clasped his hands behind his head and stretched. Rosa was restless in her sleep. Shouldn't he get up to close the curtain?

When they returned to their hometown, three families were occupying their house. They had to stay with relatives. A house was hard to find. Everyone tried to help. They had a choice between temporary housing until something more permanent became available or a house in a town nearby. They chose the latter. It was a small house. In the beginning Rosa had occasionally asked about sleeping arrangements for when the children came back. He did not know what to say. She looked at him for a long time.

"Just you wait," she said, "one day they'll suddenly stand in front of us. Jacques was never as strong as Stella, but he'll rely on his wits. And there is no doubt about Stella, she's in great physical shape."

He did not dare look at her while she spoke. He knew she didn't believe her own words. She said it for him, both to delude herself and to ease some of the tension between them, or simply to say the names once again, as in the old days. He always watched when Stella played in a tennis tournament. In the summer before mobilization she had beaten a famous English player. "That girl is fantastic," the man next to him in the stands had said. "She is my daughter." "Then I must congratulate you." That same summer

Jacques had passed his exams and had gone to study economics in Rotterdam.

They did not come back. Neither did the other relatives.
The letters from the Red Cross said so indisputably. Still,
they had gone to look at the lists that had been posted at the
office. With his finger he traced the columns. To him it was
only a question of recognition, to discover familiar names,
even if they were on the list of those who wouldn't come
back. Nothing was left of the sizable Jewish community in
their hometown. The small number of young people who
had survived had illegally moved to Palestine. But the void
created by their absence provided such a strong pull that he
was unable to resist it. He went there regularly by bus. He
told Rosa he had to take care of business. Of course he had
to start thinking about his business again. Vriens, who had
kept things running during the occupation, had already visited him a few times. When he heard everything was going
just fine, he felt more or less superfluous. In the old days he
would never have considered leaving matters to others; he
wanted to be involved in everything; nothing happened
without his knowledge. But now he hesitated as he stepped
off the bus. Should he go to his office? Occasionally he did,
but most of the time he walked the other way. He was
searching for points of reference, houses, streets, stores. One
day he visited the old synagogue. It had been turned into a
warehouse. And the house next door, where the rabbi used
to live, was now a business establishment.

He remembered the Shabbat mornings, the men in their
high hats shaking hands at the entrance, the muffled voices
in the foyer. He was standing at his bench with the prayer

shawl around his shoulders, and his hands were resting on
the wooden ledge in front of him. He smelled the leathery,
sweet scent and looked up, to Rosa and the other women
behind the partition. At the front steps a van stopped. A
man in overalls walked to the main entrance, which opened
only on special occasions, when there was a wedding or
when the chief rabbi was visiting. The door flew back and
slammed against the wall, its hinges screeching. Another
man carried a pile of boxes from the van. He looked past
them inside. Worktables designed for packing were placed
in the empty hall. The back wall, where once the holy ark
had stood, was now covered with scaffolding. He walked to
the side entrance. Crates were piled against the wall. That
wall bordered the rabbi's garden. Sometimes, when he had
to be in the conference room behind the synagogue, he could
hear the rabbi's children playing in the garden. Stella had
often been with them. When she sat on the swing he could
see her face over the wall. She would call out to him and he
would wait until she ascended again. With her head forward
and her hair flying in the wind, they would wave to each
other. He entered the lobby and asked one of the men:

"What kind of business is this anyway?"

"A paper wholesaler. Van Resema."

"Has it been here long?'

"Long? No, not really, a few years. There used to be a Jewish church here."

"Oh, yes."

"Are you looking for somebody?"

He said no and walked on, along the street beneath the
big tower, where the wind was always blowing, past Sam-
som's dry-goods store, now a bicycle repair shop, and

Meier's drugstore, also taken over by somebody else. He went in and asked for a roll of peppermints. A thin woman in a white apron waited on him. He slowly took out his wallet. He wanted to ask the woman something. She held out her hand. Suddenly he was having trouble sorting out his coins. Pretending he had something in his eyes, he simply handed her a guilder. While she made change, she turned to somebody who had come up behind her and now stood next to her behind the counter. He walked across the square where the dairy market used to be. The butter hall was now used as a rehearsal room for the local marching band, so he had been told. They had managed to keep most of the instruments out of German hands and now wanted to perform again as soon as possible. And why not? Now and then he ran into acquaintances. At first he stopped to talk to them. But the conversations varied little. Later he tried to avoid them.

"Hey, Mr. Goldstijn, you're back!"

Then he would say yes.

"How are you?"

He would say he was fine.

"And your wife and children?'

He would say his wife was fine too. The children. He shook his head. A momentary silence. Then they would ask about the other relatives from the town. Again he shook his head.

"Do you still live on the Singel?"

He told them he no longer lived in town, but in D., where they were quite comfortable. And then they would give their regards to Rosa.

Around the corner was the post office, where he used to

pick up his mail on Sunday mornings. And across the
bridge was the Singel. After initial visits with neighbors, he
had avoided this bridge. Now he crossed it, walked along
the embankment, and looked at the house where he had
lived for more than twenty years. Lace curtains in front of
the windows, potted plants, a flower box. The wood had
been painted brown. It used to be white, he thought, but he
wasn't sure. It left him cold. He turned toward the water,
where a duck was swimming now, followed by five little
ducklings. As he leaned against a tree, he looked at the
house again. He scanned it from porch to gable and felt he
was somebody else, not the man who used to live there, who
had witnessed the birth of his children behind those windows, had seen them grow, had hummed along with their
jazz records, danced at parties with his daughter's girl-
friends. Was he that same man? Better not stay too long, it
would draw attention. At the end of the Singel he crossed
the road. He walked back along the houses. He passed the
house of his friend Alex and did not understand: of this
house he recognized everything. The green stained glass in
the upper windows, the enamel plate with the house number of which the 8 was still so badly damaged that it looked
more like a 3. The copper knob of the bell. The cracks in
the concrete threshold. On the door of his former house he
saw three nameplates: two near the bell. The top one said:
W. Witgans. Below it a card: ring 3x. Doorman was the
name of the other occupant. The third had attached his
nameplate above the mailbox: L. Spijking. He knew none
of them.

On the day he had closed the door behind him for the last
time, he said to Rosa: we'll be back in a year, maybe sooner.

Rosa had left the house the way she did when they would leave for a week or so. She checked everything: whether the stove and the main faucet had been turned off, whether the window in the hallway was properly latched. In the kitchen she stopped in front of the cabinet with a package of biscuits in her hand, until he called her and she put it back into the bin. Without looking back they and their companion had walked along the Singel, to the station.

Several times he had also visited the café on the market square, which he used to frequent with Alex. Nothing had changed. Only the beer smell was more pungent, he thought. The waiter who brought his coffee acted if he had been gone no more than a month. He asked about his wife and children, where they had been hiding, how business was going. It was the same everywhere. But he continued wandering through town as if he were looking for something, as if he expected to meet someone one day who would come up to him and tell him something completely different, something he would understand. He paused by the house where one of Rosa's sisters used to live. A corner house on a boulevard across a meadow. She had been a librarian and never married. A witty woman with whom he enjoyed talking. The front yard was neglected. It was full of plants and stacks of brick, with grass and weeds sprouting up between them.

Saturday mornings he walked home with Alex. They discussed the service, the texts the cantor had used, how he had sung that morning. They had gone to the same school and continued living in the same town. They had consulted each other on business matters, and helped each other with financial problems. With Alex he would have been able to talk about it, all the things that were left unsaid between Rosa and himself, the subject they intentionally avoided. But maybe it had been recorded somewhere in just a few words. Perhaps the Talmud contained a text that alluded to it and which in turn would lead to the answer to the why that wouldn't leave him alone and that he felt might never let go of him.

One morning he went into the city park, to the small restaurant by the pond. When the children were little they had often sat down here. Stella and Jacques always immediately ran to the playground. It was chilly; the sky was gray. There were only a few children on the grounds. They were playing in the sandbox. A mother with a woolen scarf around her head sat on the concrete edge smoking a cigarette. The cold did not seem to bother the toddlers. They eagerly filled their little buckets, made mud pies, and built a small mound, as his children had done, as he himself had once done, under the watchful eye of his mother.

"Mr. Goldstijn! How are you! So long since I last saw you!"

A tall man with a goatee came toward him. He did not recognize him. But he did not let on. He pointed to the seat across from him and offered coffee. While they were talking he realized that this was Mr. Visser, the music teacher, who had taught Stella and Jacques to play the piano.

"I thought about you just last week! What a coincidence!"

"Yes, that is a coincidence."

"I happened to hear, you see, that you no longer live on the Singel."

"No, we don't. We now live in D."

"Not such a bad place, very quiet."

They usually said "not such a bad place," and he sensed a certain chauvinism in that. It irked him.

"You remember coming to our house when the students gave a recital? Your son was very talented. He was my best student."

He nodded and said he remembered.

"We still live in the same house." Mr. Visser tapped his bony fingers on the table. "When I returned I was rather surprised to find my wife still living there."

"How so? Had you been gone?"

"Yes, you didn't know? One year in the internment camp of Vught and a year in Buchenwald." He laughed. Red blotches had appeared on his gaunt cheeks. "So it goes." He stirred his coffee. His gray beard touched the edge of his cup. That emaciated face, that beard. No wonder he hadn't recognized him immediately. They drank their coffee, without another word. He sensed a similarity between this silence and the one at home. After a while he said:

"Are you teaching again?"

"Definitely. I am starting a music school here. I have always wanted to do that."

"How was it, there?"

Mr. Visser looked past him. "I think about it as little as possible. At least I try not to. It's not so easy."

He got up.

"I'd better be off."

He watched the skinny man as he left with somewhat shaky steps, as if his nervous system had been damaged. The sun broke through and lit up the table. When he went outside a child was standing in the entrance with both hands full of sand.

"Would you like a mud pie?"

He was expected to accept.

"Thank you very much," he said.

With the moist sand in the palm of his hand he walked past the pond, along the path with the benches. On the arched bridge he spotted a woman. It was too late to turn around. He prepared to answer the questions. She walked toward him.

"I thought you were at the office."

"Rosa, what are you doing here?"

"I could ask you the same thing."

He let the sand run through his fingers, rubbed his hands on his coat, and took her by the arm.

"Have you been here before?"

"A few times. But never for very long. I always had to go back one bus earlier than you."

"Have you been everywhere?"

She nodded. "And I met quite a few people who knew me."

"What did you talk to them about?"

"I don't talk to them all that much. Of course they ask all kinds of questions. They want to know everything in detail."

"I know what you mean. Would you like to live here again?"

They walked across the little bridge. He gently nudged her going up and braced her going down. She wore a black winter coat with a big collar. Black used to make her look young.

"No. We live quite well out there, don't you think? And we can go back every now and then, if we want."

"Do you feel the need to see everything again?"

"Sometimes. Then I go to the Singel, through the inner city streets. I look at the houses and stop in front of shops."

"And then you imagine how it used to be?"

"I try to see how it looks today."

"Why? To compare?"

"Because we came back. Because everything simply goes on."

Had she somehow progressed further than he, or did it just seem like that? Strange how they had never run into each other before. He wanted to say something about the dismantled synagogue, about her sister's house, and about Mr. Visser, who had been in several camps, but instead he said:

"You are right. Shall we take the bus back together?"

"Yes, let's do that."

They left the park and walked toward the bus stop. When somebody greeted them with the intention to stop, they simply answered the greeting and walked on.

He looked at his watch. It was almost half past one. What kept the neighbor in the shed all this time? They really should not keep such a distance from everybody, especially from their neighbors. The woman actually seemed quite nice to him. Why not chat with them sometime? Over a garden wall words come easy enough. And there is always some pretext: the weather, the plants, the new lawn mower he had ordered, the condition of the tomatoes, many of which had now sprung up, too many for the two of them.

It would be a shame to have to throw them out. Food and drink. Everything is available again. Nature takes its course, things come up from the ground, return to it, and sprout again.

It was quiet now down below. The light was still burning. Could he have gone to bed forgetting to turn it off? He raised his head and listened if the man was still there. He heard something. He sat up straight, his hands on the cover.

"Rosa," he whispered, "Rosa, did you hear that?'

Now he could hear it clearly. The neighbor was whistling. He whistled something that at one time had haunted him every day. A few lines he knew: "Die Fahne hoch, die Reihen fest geschlossen, S.A. marschiert." Strange how one remembers such words. The whistling sounded muffled, almost hissing, as if it was not supposed to be heard by anyone. Why would that man whistle the Horst Wessel song in the middle of the night? He was getting warm, sweat appeared on his forehead, on his neck, on his back. Did he whistle it because it simply happened to come to mind? But who would remember this particular song? The war had been over for eight years. He could be no older than his mid-thirties. An ex-Nazi, only recently released? Eight years. Then he must have been in for something serious, or maybe he had held a high function, or betrayed somebody. Could be. But people often do the strangest things when left to themselves. Thinking nobody sees or hears them, they pull faces in front of the mirror, stick out their tongue, conduct an invisible orchestra, say words they would normally not dare use, and whistle songs nobody wants to hear again, but whose melody lingers on. Quite possibly the man did not even realize what he was whistling. Why immediately think the worst?

He looked over to his wife. He was glad she had not awakened. He lay down, pulling the cover up over him. He no longer felt warm. He had to try to fall asleep. Tomorrow he would think it over one more time. He was getting upset over nothing. Tomorrow he would work things out and then it would become clear that his first reaction had been wrong. But what did it matter whether he was right or wrong? It would not change anything.

In the yard the light finally went out. The whistling continued a little while longer.

Translated by Johan Pieter Snapper

The Assault

Harry Mulisch

I

ALL THE REST IS A POSTSCRIPT—the cloud of ash that rises from the volcano, circles around the earth, and continues to rain down on all its continents for years.

In May, a few days after the Liberation, having received no news yet of Anton's parents and Peter, Van Liempt left early in the morning for Haarlem to try and find out what had happened. Apparently they had been kept under arrest, though this was not customary during such reprisals. But even if they had been taken to a concentration camp in Vught or Amersfoort, they should have been freed by now. Only the survivors of the German camps had not yet returned home.

That afternoon Anton went into town with his aunt. Amsterdam looked like a dying man who suddenly flushes, opens his eyes, and miraculously comes back to life. Everywhere flags at windowsills in need of paint, everywhere music and dancing and crowds rejoicing in the streets where grass and thistles grew between the pavement. Pale, starved people laughingly crowded about fat Canadians wearing berets instead of caps, dressed not in gray, black, or green, but in beige or light-brown uniforms that did not encase them tightly like armor, but hung loose and easy, like peacetime clothes, showing hardly any difference between soldiers and officers. Jeeps and armored cars were being patted like holy objects. Whoever could speak English not only became part of the heavenly kingdom that had come down to earth, but perhaps even received a cigarette. Boys his own age sat triumphantly on top of car radiators marked with white stars surrounded by circles. Yet he himself did not take part. Not because he was worried about his parents or Peter, for he never thought about that, but more because none of this celebration was really a part of him or ever would be. His entire universe had become that other nightmarish one that now fortunately had come to an end, and about which he never wanted to think again. Nevertheless it was part of him, so that all in all, he didn't have much left.

At dinnertime, they returned home and he went to his room, where he was quite comfortable by now. His uncle and aunt were childless and treated him as if he were their own son—or really with more consideration and less friction than if he actually had been their real child. At times he wondered what it would be like to go back to live with his parents in Haarlem, and this thought confused him so much that he quickly put it aside. He liked being at his aunt and uncle's house on the Apollolaan precisely because he did not feel like their son.

His uncle had the habit of always knocking before he entered. When Anton looked at his face, he saw at once the news he had brought. The steel clamp that had protected his uncle's pants leg on the bicycle was still around his left ankle. He sat on the desk chair and told Anton to be prepared for very sad news. His father and mother had never gone to prison. They had been shot that night, along with the twenty-nine hostages. Nobody knew what had become of Peter, so there was still hope for him. His uncle had been to the police, but they didn't know about anyone except the hostages. Then he had gone to the neighbors on the quay. No one was home at the Aartses' in Bide-a-Wee. The Kortewegs were home but refused to receive him. Finally it was the Beumers who told him the news. Mr. Beumer had seen it. Van Liempt did not go into details: Anton did not ask for any. He sat on his bed with the wall on the left, and stared down at the flamelike shapes in the gray linoleum.

He had the feeling that he had known it all along. His uncle told him that the Beumers were very glad to hear he was still alive. Van Liempt pulled the clamp off his ankle and held it in his hand. It had the shape of a horseshoe. Of course, he said, Anton would continue to live here.

Not till June did they learn that Peter too had been shot on that same evening. By then it seemed like a message from prehistoric times, hard to imagine. For Anton that distance of five months between January and June, 1945, was incomparably longer than the distance between June of 1945 and the present day. It was on this distortion of time that he later blamed his inability to explain to his children what the War had been like. His family had escaped from his memory, had retreated to a forgotten region of which he had only brief and random glimpses—as when he looked out of the window in school, or out of the rear platform on the tram—a dark region of cold and hunger and shooting, blood, flames, shouts, prison cells, hermetically sealed somewhere deep inside him. At such moments it was as if he remembered a dream, but not so much what the dream had been about, as simply the fact that it had been a nightmare. Yet at the core of that hermetic darkness now and then flashed a single source of blinding light: the fingertips of the girl caressing his face. Whether she had had anything to do with the assault, and what had happened to her, he did not know. He had no desire to know.

He finished the Gymnasium as a fair to middling student and went on to medical school. By then a lot had been published about the Occupation, but he didn't bother to read any of it, or any of the novels and stories about those days. Nor did he go to the State Institute for War Information, where he might have found out all that was known about the death of Fake Ploeg, and exactly how Peter had met his death. The family of which he had been a member had been exterminated once and for all; it was enough to be aware of this. All he knew was that the assault had never been brought to trial, for in that case he would have been questioned.

And the German man with the scar had never been tracked down. (But perhaps he had already been removed by the Gestapo. Never mind; he is the least important character in this drama.) He must have acted more or less on his own initiative. To set houses on fire in places where Nazis had been shot was not unusual, but to execute the inhabitants as well—that kind of terror had been practiced only in Poland and Russia. In those countries, however, Anton would have been killed too, even if he had still been in the cradle.

11

But things don't vanish all that easily. In September, 1952, while he was in his second year of medical school, a fellow student invited him to a birthday party in Haarlem. He had not been back since he left seven years before with the German convoy. At first he didn't plan to go, yet all day he kept thinking about it. Suddenly after lunch he grabbed a novel by a young Haarlem writer that would do for a present, though he had actually meant to read it himself, and took the tram to the station. He felt like someone going to a whorehouse for the first time.

Beyond the sandy embankment, the train passed under a huge steel pipe that was vomiting a thick, steel-gray mud onto the former peat diggings on the other side of the street. The burned-out truck had been removed. He watched the traffic on the street, his chin resting in the palm of his hand. The tram too was running again. As he passed Halfweg he saw the silhouette of Haarlem, still very much the way Ruysdael painted it—although in those days there were woods and fields where laundry lay bleaching, where Anton's house later stood. But the sky was the same: massive Alps of clouds with beams of light leaning against them. What he saw was not just any city like so many others in the world. It was as different as he himself was from other people.

Anyone watching him sitting on the pale wooden bench in third class, peering out of the compartment window of a train confiscated from the Reichsbahn, would see a twenty-year-old with sleek, dark hair that kept falling over his forehead, which he would toss back with a brief movement of the head. For some reason this gesture was attractive, perhaps because it was repeated so often that it implied a certain amount of patience. He had dark eyebrows and a smooth, nut-colored complexion, somewhat darker around the eyes. He wore gray slacks, a heavy blue blazer, a club tie, and a shirt whose pointed collar tips turned upward. The smoke that he blew with pursed lips at the windowpane clung to the glass in a thin mist for a moment.

He took the tram to his friend's house. The friend too lived in Haarlem South, but since his family hadn't moved there till after the war, they wouldn't question Anton about the past. When the tram swerved into the Hout, he caught sight for a minute of the former Ortskommandantur. The trench and barbed wire had disappeared; there was nothing left but a dilapidated abandoned hotel, its windows nailed shut. The garage (a restaurant before the War) was now in ruins. Probably his friend had no idea what kind of establishment this had once been.

"So you came after all," he said as he opened the door.

"Sorry I'm late."

"Never mind. Did you have trouble finding it?"

"Not really."

In the garden behind the house a long table stood under the tall trees. It held potato salad and other delicacies, bottles, stacks of plates, silver. On another table were the presents, to which Anton added his book. The guests stood and sat about the lawn. After he had been introduced to everyone, he joined the slightly inebriated group that he knew from Amsterdam. Holding their glasses of beer in front of their chests, they formed a circle by the edge of the water. Like Anton, they wore blazers that hung loose on their boyish frames. The leader of the group was his friend's older brother, a dentistry student in Utrecht, who wore a huge, shapeless black shoe on his right foot.

He was holding forth: "The fact is, you're all softies; that's natural. All you've got on your minds, except for jerking off, of course, is how to avoid the draft."

"That's easy for you to say, Gerrit Jan. They obviously don't want you, with that paw of yours."

"Well, I'll tell you something else, you jerk. If you had one ounce of guts, you'd not only join the army, but volunteer to go to Korea. None of you have any idea what's going on over there. The barbarians are storming the gates of Christian civilization." He wagged his index finger at them. "Compared to them, the Fascists were mere boys. Just read Koestler."

"Why don't you go yourself? Kick in their brains with that ridiculous shoe of yours, Quasimodo."

"Touché!" Gerrit Jan laughed.

"Korea is getting to be just like the University of Amsterdam," commented another. "A haven for misfits."

"Gentlemen," said Gerrit Jan, raising his glass, "let's drink to the downfall of Red Fascism, at home and abroad."

"I do keep thinking I should have joined," said a boy who hadn't picked up the drift of the conversation. "But apparently there are lots of former SS-ers in the army. I heard that if they enlist, they get off scot-free."

"So what? There's more in it than that for the SS-ers. In Korea they can really get ahead."

Get ahead, thought Anton. Really get ahead. Between two boys he peered at the opposite shore of the pond, at the peaceful lanes where people bicycled and someone was taking a dog out. Villas were there, too. Somewhat beyond them, though not visible from here, was the nursery school where he used to stand in line at the central kitchen. A bit farther and toward the left, behind the vacant lots, was the place where it had all happened. He shouldn't have come; he should never have returned to Haarlem. He should have buried all that, the way one buries the dead.

"A certain dreamer is peering into the distance," said Gerrit Jan, and when Anton looked up at him, "Yes, you, Steenwijk. Well, what's your opinion."

"What do you mean?"

"Are we going to face up to the Communists, or are we going to pussyfoot around them?"

"I've had my share," said Anton.

At that moment someone started a record on the veranda: "Thanks for the memory . . ." He smiled at the coincidence, but when he saw that the others hadn't noticed, shrugged briefly and walked away from them. The music blended with the dappled shade below the trees and somehow stirred up his memories. He was in Haarlem. It was a warm autumn day, perhaps the last one of the year, and he was once more in Haarlem. This was all wrong, and he resolved never to come back again, even if he were offered a job here at a hundred thousand gulden a year. But since he happened to be here, he wanted to say good-bye once and for all— now, immediately.

"And you, young man?"

Startled, he looked up into the face of his host. A short man with gray hair brushed to the side, wearing an ill-fitting suit with pants too short for him, as was the fashion with a certain element of the Dutch upper classes. Beside him stood his wife, a refined lady with a crooked back, so frail, all in white, that she looked as if at any moment she might fly away in a puff of dust.

"Yes, Mr. Van Lennep," he said with a smile, although he had no idea what the question was.

"Are you having fun?"

"I'm doing my best."

"Good for you. Though you don't look very happy, my friend."

"Yes," he said. "I think I'll take a tour around the block. Please don't mind me."

"Oh, we don't mind anything. Free and easy. Go ahead and stretch your legs, it clears the head."

Between tea-drinking family members sitting in white

garden chairs, he found his way into the house and out to the street. He turned into a side street and walked along the pond. When he had crossed to the other side, he looked back at the party on the lawn. The music that drifted over the water sounded even louder from here. At that moment Gerrit Jan noticed him.

"Hey, over there, Steenwijk, you asshole. The recruiting office is in the other direction."

With a wave of his hand Anton let him know that he got the joke. After that he did not look back again.

He didn't take the path across the lots, but went along the street which, around the bend, turned into the quay. This was all wrong, what he was doing; it was a mistake. "The criminal returns to the scene of the crime." With sudden excitement he recognized the herringbone pattern of the brick pavement. He had never noticed it in the old days, but now he saw it and realized that it had always been there. When he came to the water, he kept his eyes focused on the other side. The farmhands' cottages, the little farms, the mill, the meadows; nothing had changed. The clouds had vanished, the cows grazed peacefully in the evening sun. Beyond the horizon, Amsterdam, which he now knew better than Haarlem, but only in the way one knows someone else's face better than one's own.

He crossed to the sidewalk that had since been laid out along the embankment, walked on a bit, and only then jerked his face away from the water, in the other direction.

Translated by Claire Nicolas White

Apolline

Hafid Bouazza

KHADROUN STILL RUSTLES in my memory; Bertollo's grumbling has subsided, and now that Abdullah's flies no longer cloud my vision, fresh memories show me my face reflected in the murky ditch at the end of the village.

I had slipped away from my mother, who always forbade me to idle away the siesta under the carob trees by the ditch. The bearded bachelor who lived in a little white house by that same ditch had a bad name among the villagers. My mother saw my sexual stirrings as tender quarry for his allegedly unnatural proclivities (Mother, if only you knew).

But it was he who fished me out of the water when I tripped over some unremembered obstacle and fell into the ditch. He took me into his house and bundled me into a large grimy towel. And while I waited to get dry I noticed that the walls of his dwelling were papered all over with pictures of naked women, with curved cleft forms, with fair hair and parted lips. I saw mossy deltas, dusky shadows, roseate berries of flesh. These were bound to be the munificent Sirens of the Occident, and in my heart at that very moment the seeds were sown of my love for Apolline, in whom I was to find tangible evidence of that two-dimensional voluptuousness. I loved her even before I saw her.

Apolline, my will o' the wisp, my heart's fancy. How odd that a name can acquire a taste on the tongue. This taste— I know it—is physically determined, the taste of Apolline's womanhood: the taste and pungency of oyster sauce.

At first she was Abouline in my mouth; during the halting ascent of sexual peaks (which she would not allow to be wordless) she was Appelin. But now she is Apolline, she will always be Apolline, a whisper above the widening eddies of a moist death.

I can no longer recall my first impression of Amsterdam, grafted as I am on to the vertebrae of her cobbles, the wooden wombs of her bars and weathered loins of her seedy neighborhoods. I moved into a small flat in Eglantine Street: a cavity in a row of decaying teeth. It was a room with all the poetry of a solitary life: dented saucepan, unmade bed, dusty windowpanes. Single-handed solace in the tedious gloom, love at a price on Fridays. It was not long before I met Apolline.

Taller than I, blond, high-cheekboned, bushy-lashed, full-hipped, she was the perfect embodiment of my first, lonely golden summer in Vondel Park. She had an airy self-confidence that was unassailable. She sat at the table resting a cheek on her rosy palm, collarbones bare, smiling faintly. She shot me a glance from under her eyebrows, drew back her shoulders, jutted her round breasts, uncrossed her legs.

Soon Apolline detached herself from the framework of my shallow reverence. Her personality began to dominate my world.

For one thing, she would not have me perform my prayer duties in her presence. My devotion and loyalty to a religion were meaningless to her. She scoffed, wishing to divest me of what was to me my identity but to her merely the beads and the henna tracery of folklore. She wasn't having it, she was imperious, she was all woman.

She showed me Amsterdam, a naked, omnivorous, much-loved overbearing city. She was proud to walk with me at her side: those were the days when we emigrants still had a certain exotic appeal. Each walk began with a drink in a small café in a nameless alley, an oasis of bicycles and bin liners and urinated writing on the wall. (The infinitely feminine gesture of feeling for her purse in her shoulder bag.)

The Amsterdam of blue jeans, tight shirts, canals: my memory sees the city of that time in the muted shades of an eight-millimeter film. The canals dimpled and swayed with our reflections in dun-colored water, transforming us and the city and the sky into lugubrious ghosts.

She paused by a fountain and said pensively, "Funny how water always sounds so inviting. But you'd know all about that, wouldn't you, son of the dead desert?" I wonder if the last bit was a quotation.

I can still remember the briny sweetness of my first taste of pork, the acrid shudder of my first sip of wine. I remember my first drunkenness when I broke down and wept in anonymous remorse and she consoled me in her own way: my sniveling, tearful thrusting in her luxurious confines drove her to outermost abandon.

She believed I was in need of sexual re-education. Not that I was wholly inexperienced in the world's oldest rhythm

and ritual, but the way Apolline saw it I came from a country where sex served for procreation and where aphrodisiac
contortions prior to penetration were not in the cards.
These are her words. She could be so hurtful in her frivolous intelligence and breezy cynicism.

I often watched her reading magazines in which women
complained and cooed unashamedly over debacles and
delights in bed. She read them with conspicuous amusement
and approval—purely, so I thought, to hurt my feelings. *My
boyfriend wants us to get into all sorts of weird positions. Is it all
right if I swallow it?* Apolline made me read them all. *My
boyfriend has never touched me there* (Apolline: "Get this—
their advice is:") *Tell your boyfriend this is the twentieth century we're living in; you must stand up for your rights.*

She always threatened (in jest, I hope) to send off a detailed
letter if I proved unwilling to satisfy her whims (what else can
I call them?) and forswear my ethnic pride and primitive
principles. Adjusting to a new homeland, she said, had to
start, rather literally, from the bottom. She wouldn't take no
for an answer: she was so domineering, so uncontradictable,
so vibrant, so womanly. So I gave myself up—reluctant, dragging my feet, with dark circles under my eyes.

I remember the first time she made me kiss her Venus
shell. She lay spread-eagled beneath me, eyes misted over,
hair fanning out like the seaweed tresses of a water nymph.
Ali Baba was about to open the cave when she stopped me.
She steered my head southward with considerable vigor: I
resisted. In the course of an ungainly choreography a skir-
mish ensued, during which we became so entangled that I
could no longer distinguish my limbs from hers. The beast
with two backs, a multi-limbed monster. But she was
unfazed by my protestations.

In the end I gave in and it was a great relief not to have to kiss dark cockscomb lips: her Botticellian complexion found a warmer, rosier match in her young core. Her face after a sticky finale was entirely flushed, radiant, and she fixed me with a look of almost mocking triumph, which made me sad because it told me how self-absorbed her world of love and sensory pleasures was.

I do not know if she ever realized how my heart ached when I left her side to rinse my mouth and returned with dead loins that she would be at pains to kindle anew.

These are moments in my dark anguished memory (as I am now, unshaven, Apolline-less, hankering) that are suffused with brightness, sunshine even, as if my memory is trying to compensate for the weak light of the bedside lamp. I have more such memories: I am a Bluebeard's castle for the daughters of my memory.

"Ah my beloved Humayd Humayd. Outside my hotel room, somewhere in the narrow streets of Fez, a muleteer is yelling so loudly that I can barely hear myself think. Here I am in your country, and it looks disappointingly like the postcards. The other day I saw an old man squatting in the shade of a palm tree. When I asked him what he was doing there he said, Just squatting. His reply brought on what you might call a culture shock. I think I understand you better now. That is how you will undergo my love: if you're going to squat, why not under a palm tree? I have always refused to believe that there's nothing behind your inwardness. Who cares? I love you."

A letter from Apolline. She came home kissed by the southern sun, more Apollinish than ever. God knows how many pregnant men she left behind. But she reacted to my jealousy and suspicions with a shrug of her shoulders.

I had not thought she would actually go to Morocco. The way she talked was always frivolous and each time she mentioned a trip to my "fatherland" I thought she was joking. But she did go off one day, unannounced, and I still think it was one of her jokes.

To think of her pink and gold beauty in the dust and glare of that noisy, intractable country, of her clean elegance baking in that unmerciful climate.

Oh she had her good moments, moments of tenderness unswayed by the words. Sometimes she would lean with her hands on the window sill and stare outside in silence, her back arched panther-like; sometimes she would raise her shoulders and fold her shoulder blades. Or she would lie naked on the bed on her stomach reading a magazine, twirling her socked feet in the air, and now and then she would glance over her shoulder at my pointless occupations, and it was at such times that I saw the ditch again and the bearded bachelor dozing in the midday heat in front of his whitewashed abode.

At other times she would lie on her back, asleep, an upturned palm beside her warm cheekbone, lips slightly parted, the nacreous sheen of the bedside lamp playing on her ribs, thighs divided by a long dark delta. At such times she was my Apolline, more than during the livelong day.

Or she would sprawl on my chest, trace my lashes with a fingernail and say: "I can see myself in your eyes." I could see myself in her eyes, too—foreshortened, deformed, no less puny than I always felt when I was with her.

Apolline lay in bed smoking, ghosts of blue smoke coiled in the lamplight. She drew on her cigarette and stopped halfway, coughed and said: "It's flooding out. Could you get me a towel!"

The rumpled bedclothes exuded a soft aroma.

She laid her head on the pillow and said: "Apolline is the name of one of the three gods who, in the Middle Ages, were said to be worshiped by the Moors. The other two were Mahound and Termagaunt. It's amusing to think my name derives from Apollo, but it doesn't, my sweet. My name comes from Apolloyon, also known as the Destroyer, another name for the devil."

She sighed and stubbed out her cigarette. It was not unusual for her to speak to me in a patronizing tone.

She turned to me smiling, ran her eyes over my body and said: "You take your time to recover, don't you my sweet?"

What I resent is not being able to bring Apolline—she gleams like a watermark behind all my sentences, behind my existence, if you will—to life in my self-wrought language. She always eluded my grasp. Apolline was full of life, her mind latched on to each rumor in the far corners of life, she was wrapped up in it, while my own life followed a mechanical rhythm.

It is only in the photographs that I took of her and that decorate my walls that she is whole: anywhere else and she is fragmented in my memory.

On my drunken lurchings across Amsterdam I keep thinking I see Apolline. Her words, the shake of her hair, and the tap of her heels are the seams of recognition that hold the city together for me.

Distorted in the moist corners of my eyes the light of the street lamp seems to reach out for Apolline's blond hair, a peal of anonymous laughter in a smoke-filled café echoes Apolline's laugh in the dim grottos of my emotion. The girl behind the bar, her coppery hair catching the golden light, looks at me with living eyes (two glasses brimming with Dutch gin) and long-lashed tenderness, her baroque lips curled to expose young teeth. Tears of self-pity drip, drip, drip into my glass. Startled and repelled, she moves away.

Transparent clouds in the midnight-blue sky billow and curve like Apolline's contours under the pale sheet during her restive sleep. Red-framed sirens beckon behind deaf glass to me, wearing the same lingerie I wished Apolline would have worn had she not hated it.

Dark-bricked, grimy Amsterdam swaggers and staggers alongside my youthful mirror image in the murky ditch under the carob trees, where, reversed in watery reflection, the trees take on the shapes of tall, step-gabled canal houses jostling with the ruins of lives—plastic rubbish bags, bicycle carcasses—and where the sun cannot reach the naiads languishing under the rippled surface.

The blistering deathly quiet of the afternoon siesta, the dusty footpaths and the olive trees, the clamor of my disorderly childhood, these provide the background to a life in Amsterdam with rare golden summers in Vondel Park, rainy Sundays, carefree boredom, lavish twilights—they constitute the difference I shared and will forever share with Apolline.

Translated by Ina Rilke

Contributors

MANFRED WOLF, Professor Emeritus of English at San Francisco State University, has written widely on Dutch literature for such publications as *Comparative Literature, World Literature Today,* and *Saturday Review.* He has translated five volumes of Dutch poetry. An excerpt from his forthcoming memoir about growing up in the Netherlands West Indies was published in *The Beacon Best of 1999.*

∼

J. BERNLEF (b. 1937), pseudonym of Henk Marsman, has written poetry and fiction. His fictional study of an Alzheimer's patient, *Hersenschimmen,* was published in English as *Out of Mind* (1988). His novel *Public Secret* appeared in English in 1989.

MARION BLOEM (b. 1952) was born in the Netherlands of Indonesian parents. She has directed films, written for television, and produced fiction for adults and young adults. She is also a painter. Her best-known novel, *Geen Gewoon Indisch Meisje* (1983), centers around the split between her Indonesian and Dutch heritage. "A Pounding Heart" has not been published before, either in Dutch or English.

HAFID BOUAZZA, born in 1970 in Morocco, was seven when his family moved to the Netherlands. A teacher and translator of Arabic, Bouazza received a major literary prize for his first novel, *De Voeten van Abdullah*, published in English as *Abdullah's Feet* (2000).

MARTIN BRIL (b. 1959) now writes his column in the place Simon Carmiggelt (see below) had in the Amsterdam newspaper *Het Parool*. He has published two collections of columns.

REMCO CAMPERT (b. 1929) is one of the Netherlands' most prominent poets, also known for his columns and his experimental novels, two of which have appeared in English, *No Holds Barred* (1965) and *The Gangster Girl* (1968). Two collections of his poetry have also been published in English, *In the Year of the Strike* (1968) and *This Happened Everywhere* (1997).

SIMON CARMIGGELT (1913–1987) can be credited with originating and developing the column as a literary genre in the Netherlands. He wrote short sketches and columns for fifty years, and his popularity never waned.

MAARTEN 'T HART (b. 1944) was trained as a biologist but became a best-selling novelist (his recent novel *Het Woeden der Gehele Wereld* has sold 300,000 copies in Germany alone). He has also published essays on music.

BAS HEIJNE (b. 1960) is a novelist, critic, and prize-winning translator (from English). "Flesh and Blood" comes from his 1995 short story collection *Vlees en Bloed*.

GERRIT KOMRIJ (b. 1944) is a poet, essayist, playwright, fiction writer, and translator. In 1999, Komrij was named poet laureate of the Netherlands.

HERMINE LANDVREUGD (b. 1967) was born in the Netherlands of a Surinamese father and a Dutch mother, a background reflected in some of her work. She is the popular author of three volumes of short stories and a screenplay, and has recently published a book for children.

GEERT MAK (b. 1946) is best known as a nonfiction writer, whose *Amsterdam: A Brief Life of the City* (1999) and *Jorwerd: The Death of the Village in Late–Twentieth Century Europe* (2000) have recently been published in English.

LIZZY SARA MAY (1918–1988) is the author of several novels and short story collections, among them *Vader en Dochter*. "Zakendoen" ("Business") was first published in *Oom Bennetje Raaskalt* (1987). She also wrote extensively for Dutch television.

MARGA MINCO (b. 1920) is the author of *Het Bittere Kruid* (1957; in English *Bitter Herbs,* 1960) and many other novels. An English translation of her story, "The Return," was published in *Women Writing in Dutch* (1994).

HARRY MULISCH (b. 1927) is best known in the English-speaking world for his widely praised novels, *The Assault* (1986), *Last Call* (1989), and *The Discovery of Heaven* (1996). He is generally regarded as one of Holland's most prominent post–World War II authors and has created an enormous body of work, consisting of fiction, nonfiction, and poetry.

CEES NOOTEBOOM (b. 1933) has an international reputation, with many novels translated into English. His best-known work in English is probably *Rituals* (1983), but many other novels have a significant following in several countries. He is also widely known for his travel writing, his most recent being the award-winning *Roads to Santiago* (1997).

GERARD REVE (b. 1923) was born in Amsterdam as Gerard Kornelis van het Reve. His first novel, *De Avonden* (1947), was an enormous success in the post–World War II era. Since then, he has published highly regarded fiction, some of it confessional and epistolary. His novel *Parents Worry* came out in English translation in 1991. The English translation of "The Decline and Fall of the Boslowits Family" was first published in *The Literary Review* (Winter, 1961–62).

J.J. VOSKUIL (b. 1926) published his first novel, *Bij Nader Inzien,* in 1963 and remained silent for over three decades. Then, starting in the mid-nineties, he published volume after volume of a massive novel, *Het Bureau,* which renders in painstaking detail the workings and intrigues of an Amsterdam office. Seven volumes have now been published to great acclaim in the Netherlands.